PRAISE FOR *DIQUE DOMINICAN*

"These times demand such acts of courage and skill."
—Ana Castillo, author of *The Mixquiahuala Letters, So Far From God, and Massacre of the Dreamers: Essays on Xicanisma*

"*Dique Dominican* is a candid, often moving account of what it was like for a Dominican-American to grow up in East New York . . . His story takes us back to his childhood in a small farm town near Juncalito, about 160 kilometers north of Santo Domingo, records his life in his hood and his move to Ohio in order to continue with his studies. As the author illustrates his family dynamics, the reality of his community, and his attempt to negotiate his way between English and Spanish, sharing with us, at the same time, his personal trajectory, ambitions, and reflections, Ayendy Bonifacio always keeps his own lucidity in front of pain, discrimination, and violence. Never overstated, his account is like a whisper which, however, forcefully demands to be heard."
—Maria Cristina Fumagalli, author of *Caribbean Perspectives on Modernity: Returning Medusa's Gaze* and *On the Edge: Writing the Border Between Haiti and the Dominican Republic*

"Language is home—and isn't. It makes room for us, allowing us comfort. Or it proscribes us, sending us into the vertigo of exile. In *Dique Dominican*, [Bonifacio] gets lost and found as he navigates the interstices where words struggle for meaning. A courageous, Babel-like journey!"

—Ilan Stavans, author of *On Borrowed Words: A Memoir of Language* and general editor of *The Norton Anthology of Latino Literature*

"A striking account of his journey from the campo in the Dominican Republic to Brooklyn to Ohio, as well as an exploration of independence and transcendence. The vivid details in this memoir portray more than the disparate places traversed, they reveal Bonifacio's own complex internal landscape. Intense, honest and bold."

—Erika M. Martínez, editor of *Daring to Write: Contemporary Narratives by Dominican Women*

Dique Dominican

AYENDY BONIFACIO

This work is a piece of creative nonfiction, broadly interpreted.
Elements of fiction are interwoven with the memories, experiences,
narratives, and details presented within these pages. These might be
characterized as autofictions or perhaps as inevitable outcomes of the
inherent imperfections of memory and human perception. It is
sufficient to say that, at some point, these accounts were inspired by a
version of the truth.

Attention schools and businesses: for discounted copies on large
orders, please contact the publisher directly.

For information contact:
Unsolicited Press
Portland, Oregon
www.unsolicitedpress.com
orders@unsolicitedpress.com
619–354–8005

Cover Design: Joey S. Kim
Editor: Summer Stewart

ISBN: 978-1-963115-67-3

For my loves, Joey and Evie

ACKNOWLEDGMENTS

Let me be honest with you, I used to hate writing acknowledgments. The word always felt too clunky, nearly impossible to spell. And, of course, what followed was the difficult task of briefly describing the brilliance and generosity of so many people in so few words, mind you, after the exhausting completion of the project itself. Then there was the risk of sounding glib and so well-rehearsed that your words of thanks mean very little. But I've grown, reader. Age has taught me a little patience, and patience is a quirky thing. So, allow me to be weird in my expression of gratitude so as to not appear bitter and tired.

Brief as they may be, I want these acknowledgments to be the symbolic giving-of-flowers to the hands that have pulled me through to this moment. There are many hands. Some might get a wilting rose or a dry leaf. Some might get nothing, and that's my bad.

Many of the stories in this book are about family in this realm and otherwise. If I've ever had a conversation with you about growing up, family, coffee, and/or the Caribbean, thank you. Your words were neatly folded and stowed in the bureau of my thoughts. Thank you to my grandparents, Mamá Flora and Papá Victor, for holding my hand through life. Your voices are in every line of this book. Thank you to my parents, Mami y Papi, for your devotion to keeping me and my siblings alive and well. Now that I'm a parent, I understand more than ever that you did your best. I will always translate your love and joy, your aches and regrets, for they are my own.

Thank you to my sister, Jessica Bonifacio, for reminding me to stay grounded in joy and gratitude. Your daily phone calls feel like *bachata* with *cafécito* on 52 Sunnyside Ave. Thank you to my brother, Estarly Bonifacio, for your creativity and energy for your life and family. I want to hand out flowers to all of you: Isaura Bonifacio, Ángel Bonifacio, Isabella Bonifacio, Ramon Ulloa, Reynaldo Ulloa, Omar Ulloa, Cristobal Ulloa, Drs. Hyo Kim, Jin Kim, Jennifer Kim, and Victor Pham, thank you. To Adeline Pham, Sophia Pham, Christine Kim, Jonah Gold, Haven Gold, Esther Kim, Joseph Familia, Ruben "Gugy" Cedeño, Mark "Mikey" Cedeño, José Castillo, Jonathan Santana, and Mike Loubriel, every conversation, hug, and shared time is a breath of life. All your spirits have carried me to this moment and given me strength and motivation.

Sincerest thanks to the writers, artists, teachers, mentors, and lifelong friends I have been able to work with and learn from while writing this book. Thank you, Ana Castillo, Elizabeth Renker, Carol Oliver, Eduardo C. Corral, Kathy Fagan, Fior E. Plasencia, Ilan Stavans, Maria Cristina Fumagalli, Erika M. Martínez, Jessica Hong, Angela Abreu, Torsa Ghosal, Jason Schneiderman, Christina Lam, Nita Noveno, Jamie Lyn Smith, and Marcus Jackson. Your words have kept me climbing, gripping, and pulling myself up to something like getting better.

To my UToledo gang, Joseph Gamble, Adam Wagner, Dustin Pearson, thank you. Joey G. and Adam, I love seeing the life that you are creating. Thanks, Dustin Pearson, for pastries and poetics, the smiles and photos. Thank you to

Kim Mack, Parama Sarkar, Andrew Mattison, Tina Fitzgerald, Ben Stroud, Dan Campora, Tyler Branson, Tim Geiger, Natalie Bullock, Mel Gregory, Karie Peralta, Charles Beatty-Medina, and Charlene Gilbert. You have all pushed me to be a better writer, thinker, and educator. I am grateful for your support and collegiality.

I would also like to thank all of my co-collaborators, creative and academic friends, colleagues, and thinkers who supported this book from the start in one way or another Thank you to the generous and amazing mentors, teachers, colleagues, and collaborators who have guided me along the way: Lorgia García Peña, Eduardo C. Corral, Jewon Woo, Eric Gardner, Rodrigo Lazo, Jesse Alemán, Elisa Sampson Vera Tudela, Kenya Dworkin, Carmen Lamas, Robert McKee Irwin, Jean Lee Cole, Bernadine Hernandez, Karen R. Roybal, Mark Noonan, Kelley Kreitz, Adam McKible, Jesse W. Schwartz, Daniel Worden, Trent Masiki, Justin Mann, Emily Hainze, Travis Foster, Brigitte Bailey, Renee Hudson, Maia Gil'Adí, Sarah Salter, Jim Casey, Michael Dowdy, Janet Neary, Red Washburn, and so many others. You have all shaped my thinking, reading, and writing in significant ways. Thank you and thanks again for your generosity, mentorship, and friendship—for motivating me to keep *writing and rewriting a lot of this book.*

Sincerest thanks to Unsolicited Press editor, Summer Stewart, for giving *Dique Dominican* a new home and life.

Lastly, to my hearts—the spur of my love and inspiration—my partner, Joey S. Kim, and our daughter, Evie Arum Kim-Bonifacio: you both fill my life with meaning and care. Evie, you have taught me to love the way only fathers can. Every day with you is the best day of my life. My better half and co-conspirator, Joey S. Kim, we have been many different types of people together: students, professors, writers, and now parents. What remains consistent is your love of words and family. Our evening walks that turn into debates, seminars, poetry readings, and rap battles rejuvenate the deepest parts of my spirit. Thanks for making all of us feel a little more at home.

PUBLISHER'S NOTE

This book uses Dominican Spanish and American English spelling throughout, with footnotes translating Dominican Spanish to American English.

ALSO BY AYENDY BONIFACIO

Paratextuality in Anglophone and Hispanophone Poems in the U.S. Press, 1855-1901

To the River, We Are Migrants

Dique
Dominican

By and by all trace is gone, and what is forgotten is not only the footprints but the water too and what it is down there. The rest is weather. Not the breath of the disremembered and unaccounted for, but wind in the eaves, or spring ice thawing too quickly. Just weather. Certainly no clamor for a kiss.

Toni Morrison[1]

I am my mother's dreams fulfilled, my grandmother's vengeance realized, patriarchy's worst nightmare, a testament to the power of anticolonial resistance. I am all they—those who stole lands and enslaved people—were afraid of and more; rebellion is my birthright.

Lorgia García Peña[2]

. . . the light brought the bitter history of sugar . . .

Derek Walcott[3]

---

[1] Toni Morrison, *Beloved* (1987)

[2] Lorgia García Peña, *Community as Rebellion: A Syllabus for Surviving Academia as a Woman of Color* (2022)

[3] Derek Walcott, "BOOK SIX," *Omeros* (1990)

PREFACE

I was a junior at Hunter College when I started writing *Dique Dominican* in 2011. I desperately wanted to become a writer, so the book's initial drafts became a sort of exercise in writing: how to structure and punctuate a sentence, how not to be afraid of words. This exercise ended up turning into a decade-long reflection on the root of my anger, the hideous part of myself—the one I was, and am, most ashamed to talk about. I noticed the detours my anger took in the Dominican section of my brain—where all my childhood memories lived, blasting merengue through the synapses—in the East New York blocks of my adolescence—where we bounced basketballs until the streetlights hummed—ending up right here. So, I wrote about those things.

My anger is mine. It is an emotion of my own carving, one that has grown strong with everyone and anyone who has crossed paths with it. It is a contagious emotion—infectious and prone to infection from others' anger—and it will be with me forever. At the same time, like anything born of this world, it has an origin. In my search, I find myself knocking on Papi's coffin.

bell hooks writes in *The Will to Change*, "My longing for my father's death began in childhood. It was the way I responded to his rage, his violence. I used to dream him gone, dead and gone."[4] My father is "dead and gone." It's the most painful truth I will offer in this book. There is nothing like the hollowness that comes with the death of a parent. It is the partial and permanent emaciation of your soul. It was after Papi's sudden death that I took hooks' words seriously. Many times, I pictured Papi's death as a child and as an adult. Every fleeting moment after his *correa* tore through my flesh, leaving the sting there, ringing with burn.[5] Every time he let me down, missing my graduation and wedding day. But like those gashes, my anger always went elsewhere.

My love for Papi always, somehow, overpowered my hate. Even when I hated him, I loved him, and vice versa. There was something in my ability to love, perhaps in how I loved, that was tied to my anger, and I wanted to uncover this for myself. hooks continues, "Women and children all over the world want men to die so that they can live. This is the most painful truth of male domination, that men wield patriarchal power in daily life in ways that are awesomely life-threatening, that women and children cower in fear and various states of powerlessness."[6] As a child, I cowered in terror of Papi's power. Years later, as a young adult, I found myself shrinking in fear of myself, of what I had become. It's perhaps my most tragic transition—going from terrified to terror. But it also seems like the only transition I could've ever made. Growing up, I didn't "bear the intimacy of scrutiny," as Audre Lorde says, of

---

[4] bell hooks, *The Will to Change* (2004)

[5] Belt.

[6] hooks, *The Will to Change* (2004)

my anger.[7] I didn't know that I could. So, when death stopped for Papi, I felt like his killer.

I never thought much about the root of my anger, much less its turbulent link to the feelings of a killer: the sense of evil, badness, and hopelessness of it all. Killing our fathers is rarely discussed outside of the Oedipus complex. Nonetheless, as hooks says, "Women and female and male children, dominated by men, have wanted them dead because they believe that these men are not willing to change. They believe that men who are not dominators will not protect them. They believe that men are hopeless." The ironic truth of being both a cisgender hetero man, and a child that was once dominated by his father, is that I am now always near becoming a hopeless gear in male domination, perhaps I already am.

I begin here, with this, because despite how it reads, I loved my father. But behind the canopy of love is a trunk of hate, the bark and crack of pain, anger, and violence that love often conceals in its shadow. I begin with this as an attempt to bear witness to the shadows of our suffering, and, most importantly, the love that shaped my anger.

The fear of Papi's power, his violent strength, a force I couldn't match, was my teacher for my own budding *machismo*. In trying to overpower and defeat him, I defeated myself. His anger became mine like some family heirloom. Even after he died, I sensed the ugliest parts of his temper within me.

My therapist tells me that anger is just like any other emotion. That it is a healthy part of our emotional response to the world. That it serves us to an extent. I tell him that anger

---

[7] Audre Lorde, "Poetry is Not a Luxury" (1984)

is the emotion I lead with. It's where I stand when faced with anything that shakes me, challenges, confuses, arrests me—anything. It's where Papi stood too. In that way, we stand together.

Papi was our protector in this new country. When we arrived, he was the cave that sheltered us in a Brooklyn basement, so humid that the walls perspired like chilled Presidentes on Summer nights. I willingly endured his whip, knowing that it came with his protection, his healing hands. Men are taught to be tough, angry, and violent, especially if it's for the protection of their family. We are told that being angry is normal; it's part of our essence, that it's our nature to be closed off to our emotions and pick ourselves up, pressing the wound. At least that's what I learned. There was always this implacable power to Papi's place in our house. His gravity, both heavy and light, unpredictable at times, and always in need of tending, felt like the only thing keeping us from disintegrating into nothing.

We, the children of the apartment, hungered for Papi's love and recognition. When Papi got home from work, my little brother and I put on a show. Sometimes it was dancing and singing. But most of the time, it was fist fighting for his attention. We wanted Papi to see us, to know us, maybe even respect us, so that we could know him. It was a unique desperation, one that we did not extend to Mami, who was the nurturer in our lives.

Papi's love was rare, it derived from his relative absence. Mami had no choice but to be around—before and after school, at parent-teacher conferences, and everywhere in between. Papi worked a lot, long hours in a different borough. But it wasn't just our Papi who had this rare valuable love. It seemed to me that my friends' fathers too had this same type of sparing love. Their fathers weren't around either. Some had died. Some were in prison. Others had left. We yearned for a role model, an Uncle Phil type, who would guide us and give shape to our masculinity.

To us boys in the hood, becoming a man meant learning something from your father. So, every minute, every beatdown and gentle caress, every joke and disciplinary shout, was a lesson. When our fathers were absent, the hood provided alternative father figures, the corner drug dealer, the hooper with the mean jump shot, the *bodeguero* who gives you a free candy when you buy groceries. In short, we wanted fathers to teach us how to protect ourselves so that we could be worthy of someone else's love.

By my sixteenth birthday, after my parents divorced, my love for Papi turned into hate. I didn't know the soft lines between these two strong emotions. Hate was easier to handle, made more sense to me as a young person learning to be a man. Hate felt like the masculine emotion to consume, the one that would make me strong and powerful, especially in my fight with my father. Hate was also going to help me block his whip, snatch it from him in a show of dominance, and deliver mercy or malice depending on how I felt. My hate found a voice in anger, rage, and grief. I closed myself off to the hand of Papi's love, and there was nothing he could do to open that door.

When Papi lay in a hospital at Memorial Sloan Kettering Cancer Center in midtown Manhattan, quickly dying from an invasive and relentless brain cancer, the soft lines between love and hate felt like a betrayal. What did it matter now? All that time I spent yearning for a specific type of love from my father, all the time I spent hating him for not being who I thought he should be? My hate and anger turned inward, and his approaching death felt like a personal failure. Somehow, someway, I was to blame for his cancer. Its growth and metastasis. What good was all that anger? Did it ever serve me? Will it betray me again?

This expanded and revised edition of *Dique Dominican* is an attempt at answering these questions. It is about what comes after the simplicity of the exclamation *Yes*. Through childhood vignettes, Dominican history and folklore, US and Caribbean racial logics, and self-reflection, this book is an exploration of how anger, hate, and love are lifelong companions of mine, whom I'm still getting to know.

After many months of editing, cutting, and rewriting a very rough manuscript, and with the help of my tireless partner, who helped give the book shape, the first edition of this book was released in 2017. I was a PhD candidate writing a dissertation about nineteenth-century newspaper poems in Columbus, Ohio, a topic and a place as far away from my childhood and young adult reality as I could imagine. Donald Trump was elected the 45th President, and my brother and I were wondering if we (me as a naturalized citizen and him as a permanent resident) were going to be deported. I was in a different state and state of mind, trying desperately to recall the past, contending with my present, but also, perhaps selfishly, trying to create a foundation for a successful future. I had two more years left in my degree program. Some of my peers were on the job market, applying to tenure-track positions across the country. Our department held mock job talks to help them practice as well as alt-ac seminars for those interested in pursuing careers outside of academia. It was a stressful time for all of us. Many of my peers didn't start tenure-track jobs. I was afraid that after spending all that time working on my PhD that I wouldn't be employed in the end.

When the first edition of *Dique Dominican* came out, I hoped it would achieve two things. First, I wanted readers to connect with a story that felt both personal and universal—about being a Dominican immigrant in East New York who falls in love with books and writing. It's a story I still consider both important and rare. Second, I hoped the book would propel my early career as a hopeful professor and writer. The precarity of the job market made me believe that publishing a book would make me stand out against the competition. For me getting a tenure track job was a contest that I needed to win. It was not a process decided by the complex often political needs of a university, the prestige of a department, nor luck. For me, it was a referendum on my identity.

There was a lot of pressure. I didn't want to move back to East New York with a fancy degree and no job prospects. So, I threw myself into publishing *Dique*, a book about the hood and *campo*, while researching and writing my dissertation, a book about textuality, nineteenth-century poets, panics, and disease.[8] I believed the job market would reward me for my unusual productivity. I was right. Two years before graduating, I applied for a tenure-track position at CUNY and, to my surprise, I got a first-round interview. The committee brought up my book as part of my record of productivity.

---

[8] Countryside.

I didn't get the job. But that interview left me with a key, I thought, that unlocked my success in this profession: record of productivity. I believed that the more I wrote and published, the more successful I would be. I took the old proverb "publish or perish" to heart. I loved writing, so turning this into an identity, I thought, was a win-win situation. I began devoting my life to a rigorous writing schedule, submitting work in all genres imaginable, sometimes mindlessly—poetry, nonfiction, scholarship, journalism, fiction, you name it. With all these submissions brought a torrent of rejections, some acceptances, but most notably, an inseverable link with toxic productivity.

There came a point where I would submit work simply to feel seen, to get recognition from my peers, to post about a publication, an award on Twitter/X for likes and reposts—for anything that would give me a sense of purpose. The writing itself, at this rate, was becoming alienating labor, like something I was doing for someone else. This writing had nothing to do with me or who I wanted to be.

There came a point when my career as an English professor was taking off while I secretly dealt with some of the worst depression and anxiety I had ever experienced. I began suffering from prolonged abdominal pain that even today remains unresolved, with the cause unknown. While teaching, my stomach turned in the middle of lectures at times stopping me mid-sentence. I thought about my mortality more often, my family health history, and whether I'd be around next year or the year after that. These thoughts became more frequent, especially as the political climate became more and more anti-Black, anti-immigrant, and anti-intellectual.

I wasn't alone in these thoughts or at least it seemed like more critics and creatives were contemplating the paradox of our work and our mental and physical health. After the death of bell hooks in 2021 at 69, many began thinking about the relationship between the rigors of academia and early or premature deaths on people of color, particularly women of color whose success as professors, mentors, administrators, and writers comes with the heavy intersectional anvil of sexism, racism, and misogyny. Before her passing, hooks published more than 30 books and, as *The New York Times* reported in her obit, "insisted that the fight for women's rights had to take into account the diverse experiences of working-class and Black women."[9] Less than two years later, Temple University Acting President JoAnne Epps suddenly died while attending a memorial service for Charles L. Blockson, a notable Black American historian of the culture of African American and African diaspora. Epps was 72. The phrase "tragic irony" is too clumsy to hold the truth of Epp's awful passing. Days after Epp's death, Dr. Orinthia T. Montague, the president of Volunteer State Community College, dies at only 56. Montague was a self-described doer, someone who got things done. She once said, "I'm the kind of leader who will volunteer to help, I'm not just asking someone else to do it."[10] On January 8, 2024, the day my daughter was born, Antoinette "Bonnie" Candia-Bailey, the vice president of student affairs at Lincoln University, committed suicide after being harrassed and bullied, according to reports, by John

---

[9] Clay Risen, "bell hooks, Pathbreaking Black Feminist, Dies at 69," *The New York Times* (2021).

[10] "Get to Know Dr. O, VOL State's Fourth President," *The Settler* (2021)

Mosefly, the white male president of the historically Black university. She was only 49. What do all these women have in common? They were Black women, successful, in positions of power, and they all died before the life expectancy for Black women which is approximately 78.1 years

Critics across Black feminist, cultural, and literary studies have long observed and analyzed how Black women are expected to do more—emotionally, physically, socially, and professionally—often without acknowledgment or support. This expectation is frequently framed as part of a broader system of racialized and gendered labor rooted in slavery, settler colonialism, and capitalist patriarchy. Audre Lorde named this plainly: "My anger has meant pain to me but it has also meant survival."[11] Her essays insist that Black women's emotional labor—especially anger—is a response to a system that consumes their care and punishes their refusal. Kandice Chuh, reflecting on institutional demands, describes how the tradition of "liberal humanities diversity" turns scholars of color into symbolic laborers, native informants called on to represent, to make visible, and to explain often without meaningful institutional transformation. Chuh posits that "As people whose scholarly genealogies are constitutively misaligned with, even as we are contextualized by, the university's role as an apparatus of the nation-state and of capital, scholars of minoritized discourses cannot and do not easily inhabit the academy."[12] bell hooks argued that the trope of the stereotypical image of the "strong Black woman" is only one "dimension" of Black women's story: "It is not that Black

---

[11] Audre Lorde, *Sister Outsider* (1984).
[12] Kandice Chuh, *The Difference Aesthetics Makes* (2013)

women have not been and are not strong; it is simply that this is only part of our story, a dimension, just as the suffering is another dimension one that had been most unnoticed and unattended to."[13] These voices, across decades, remind us that the burden placed on Black women is neither incidental nor accidental. It is historical, systemic, and ongoing.

I do not mean to equate my own feelings of pain or inadequacy with the historical and ongoing experiences of Black women and other women of color whose lives and labor have been shaped by much more violent conditions. Rather, I want to shed light on the often invisible hostility and embodied consequences of academic labor, particularly for people of color navigating institutions not built with us in mind. As I began to reckon with my own body, I found myself increasingly caught in a paradox of achievement and deterioration. The more I produced, the more I was praised, the more my mind and body faltered. I became desensitized to recognition. I had wrongly assumed that success—through publication, strong evaluations, or professional praise—would offer healing. In truth, it was the work itself that was driving me toward despair.

People of color in predominantly white industries and institutions often must work twice, if not three times, as hard as our white counterparts. We are expected to meet unrealistic standards and goals for being the first of our kind, to prove that we belong, that our existence isn't accidental, and that our roles are merited. But at what expense?

My personal relationship with work came from my parents, and the only work they knew in this country was

---

[13] bell hooks, *Talking Back: Thinking Feminist, Thinking Black* (1999)

alienating labor. We came to this country from the Dominican Republic when I was six. Papi worked many labor-intensive jobs to make ends meet. In the early '90s, he was a "delivery boy" (Papi's words) in midtown Manhattan; in the early aughts, he was a "helper" for a juice distribution company; in the last years of his life, he, in his own words, "settled down," and drove a cab. Papi took me to all these jobs, modeling for me how to make it in this country. Even on his deathbed, Papi worried about his business and customers. "The car, *mijo*," he said a week before dying, "the door needs to be repaired."

Since then, I've often wondered what door Papi was referring to. Was it the one that opened when we arrived in this country, stepping into what we believed was our American dream of work, education, and safety? Was it the door of social class—one that kept us perpetually on the outside, always brushing up against poverty? Or was it the door now closing on him, ushering him into the next realm where my grandfather had gone a year before, and where my grandmother would follow five years later, unable to cope with the loss of her last son? Whatever door he meant, one thing was certain: "The door [indeed] needed repaired."

Before immigrating to the U.S., Mami dropped out of school at 16 to help her family make ends meet as well. She was employed as a servant by a wealthy Dominican family in Santiago. When she moved to the U.S., housekeeping was the only job she could do. She worked all over Manhattan, ultimately finding purpose in this work because it provided for us. Her true passion, however, is singing, which she only does at her church. These aren't just family stories; they became a roadmap for how to survive in the world, one that I am still processing, one that hems me in even as it helped.

As the oldest of my three siblings, I became the one in my family who checked off the list of first accomplishments: first to graduate high school, first to go to college, first to get a doctorate, and first to become a professional. I did this with a sense of responsibility for my family, my students, and the future of my profession, without thinking much about my own physical and mental health. On most nights, I woke up in a pool of cold sweat, wanting to keep my pain to myself, bury it somewhere no one could find. At doctor visits, I found myself with a 10-year-old's vocabulary for speaking about my pain. My acute abdominal pain becomes a ball in my chest; my night sweats become hot sleep. When asked how much pain I have on a scale of 1-10, I nervously minimize it, answering "1 and 2." My own verbal inability perplexed me because I wrote and read for a living. My partner became my voice. She told my doctors my symptoms and took rampant notes. I listened as if they were talking about someone else in the room. I've always been taught to suck it up—to be strong and push through, to not complain, and be grateful—all the while believing that this is the measure of a good person.

The year before I earned tenure, my toxic productivity began to feel like the alienating labor I did in my twenties, standing idly for eight hours working security and the monotonous toil of moving and delivering boxes of juice across the five boroughs. I hated that work because it disconnected me from my body, my mind, and the nature of who I was. I didn't want to be a human surveillance camera making sure shoppers didn't steal from multi-billion-dollar companies or a machine that moved boxes from point A to point B. It was ironic then that my intellectual work, a work that I trained my entire career to do, was beginning to feel alienating. I was at the precipice of tenure, a monumental milestone for anyone who does this kind of work, but felt as hollow as I've ever felt.

Somehow I could not escape becoming a cog in the capitalist machinery of production. I was part and parcel of the general law of capitalist accumulation with a flare of intellectualism. As Karl Marx put it, "Accumulation of wealth at one pole is . . . at the same time the accumulation of misery, agony of toil, slavery, ignorance, brutality, mental degradation, at the opposite pole."[14] My toxic productivity turned from a means of creating career opportunities to means of being seen, admired, and loved to an accumulation of misery, anxiety, and believe it or not, anger. I was back to where I started, an angry Dominican immigrant, but no longer a boy, now an adult.

---

[14] Karl Marx, *Capital: A Critique of Political Economy, Volume 1* (1867).

1

Speech is my hammer, bang the world into shape
Now let it fall, huh!

Mos Def[15]

Language is liberation. And honestly, I don't know if I've ever truly been free. The first time I listened to Yasiin Bey's *Black on Both Sides*, I was a senior at Boys and Girls High School. I saw myself woven into his lines, not just in the music, but in the codes I'd been switching my whole life—not only between English and Spanish, but between the different voices I used in spaces that didn't leave room for me. "Young man, where you from? Brooklyn number one! / Native son, speaking in the native tongue."[16] For the first time, I started to think of my language—the blend of Dominican Spanish and Brooklyn English—as something real, something legitimate. It wasn't just a mishmash of sounds, but a full blast of language of its own, and I was fluent in it.

In many ways, my own independence came in the form of two languages, battling for legitimacy, righteousness,

---

[15] Yasiin Bey (Mos Def), "Hip Hop" *Black On Both Sides* (1999).

[16] Ibid.

perhaps even vengeance. What the battle left behind was a type of wandering, an escape even, from my anger.

It happened before the climate started warming so fast. Back then, we still had cold winters. The snow and chill were punctual, almost aligning with the holiday breaks and winter trips to DR. The trees were bare, erect like chiseled statues on the block. Its leaves collecting under sewer drains and garbage cans. Brooklyn was still a nasty place for me. The acrid taste of my high school years lingered in my mouth, the taste of blood and paranoia, a mouth full of the fact that I was destined to be a piece of shit. That night, the frigidness of the air did not change the taste of despair and anger.

Mami and I stood like perfect strangers outside the building, in front of the four-step stoop that witnessed so many loitering summers, blunt passing, Jordan scuffing, and first kisses in the yellow veil glowing, buzzing streetlight. I could feel the gaze and ears of our neighbors—fucking *metiches*—who, although likely annoyed, were not surprised that the Dominican family on the first floor were at it again, yelling and fighting like animals.[17]

Mami and I didn't know it then, but we were standing at a crossroads that would change us for the rest of our lives. One direction led to the same tired fighting and yelling, a mode of communication that Papi and Mami rehearsed daily and that my siblings and I picked up as our own. In the next three years, Mami and I would be estranged from one another. All modes of communication cut, while I figured out if I wanted to stay alive or not. Papi had already left. His violent outrage, which Mami surely matched, coupled with his young girlfriends in

_____

[17] Nosy.

34

DR, were too much for Mami. So that was that, although Papi had this hopeless desire to make things better, to make them work. That shit never passed, though.

Our bodies shivered, exhausted from the cursing and yelling, as we waited for my little sister, Julissa. This whole thing started because the waiting turned into an obituary in my head. Julissa never came home after school, and now hours had passed. Mami was near tears because of the ominous likelihoods I put in her head, the griminess of the Five Boroughs, the way they chewed on your ego and sense of self and spat you out in the image of tasteless and amorphous gum. If the city did that to me, I told Mami, what do you think it will do to a thirteen-year-old girl out in the streets on a cold December school night.

I think we both believed the worst: that she had been abducted, murdered, and was gone forever. We believed that we were the type of people for whom shit like this happened: a forgotten people building a life on top of a mound of *mierda*.[18] With each passing hour, we lost hope. It was almost midnight, and Julissa hadn't called. No one I knew on the block had seen her. This was not like Julissa. She was a straight-A student who always did as she was told. If Mami told her to be somewhere at a certain time or do something a specific way, Julissa followed those instructions with religious fervor. She was nothing like me. Instruction was a word I couldn't spell, let alone practice.

It was natural that Julissa's absence fucked me up inside. It was natural to think about the million and one things that could go wrong. The fact that it was a fifteen-minute walk

---

[18] Shit.

from Broadway Junction to our building on Sunnyside Avenue, and that on your walk home under the J train on Fulton Street, streetlights were scarce. The sidewalk shifted like tectonic plates under you as you advanced beside vacant lots and errant tree branches crawling through rusty fences that seemed to stretch towards you, asking to run your pockets until you reached a lit corner in front of the corner bodega, a checkpoint, a passing patch of safety, and then continued home.

But the word "natural" does not hold steady my response to the situation, which, in fact, was an example of my response to life back then. Anyone and anything that didn't agree with me, that got in the way of my food, money, my way, was met with anger. I was always angry. You could say that it's a part of my identity, something that even today I struggle to conceal out of shame and guilt.

The dictionary defines anger as a strong feeling of annoyance and hostility. I don't think that fully describes my anger. My anger had hands for punching and choking. My anger had a creative way of imagining how to verbally and physically induce pain on those who had wronged me. My anger was an employed torturer, with full benefits, torturing for practice, to not be forgotten. My anger ruled over my body and mind like a gluttonous dictator over a starving country.

In *The Will to Change* (2004), bell hooks writes, "There is only one emotion that patriarchy values when expressed by men; that emotion is anger. Real men get mad. And their madness, no matter how violent or violating, is deemed natural, a positive expression of patriarchal masculinity."[19]

---

[19] bell hooks, *The Will to Change* (2004).

The thing is, while I felt more masculine when I was angry, another part of me felt less human because of the people my anger hurt. How could I be so consumed by rage—rage to the point of wanting to kill, of picturing myself strangling the life out of my own mother? Was that what being a "real man" meant? If this was natural, or even a positive expression of masculinity, then the patriarchy wasn't just harming women—it was trying to kill men too, slicing away at our humanity.

hooks also writes, "Anger is the best hiding place for anybody seeking to conceal pain or anguish of spirit."[20] One of the realest things I've ever read. I hid everything in my anger, my desires, insecurities, vulnerability, ignorance, pain, even love. All of it, buried behind fists of fire, hands ready to strangle, and a mind that was slowly bleeding out. Anger made me feel powerful, but at the same time, it made me hollow— less of a man, less of a person. It wasn't strength; it was survival. And it was killing me too.

"This is all your fault," I said to Mami in my weak Spanish. "Where the fuck is she? And you know that if she's hurt, or worse yet, if she's dead, you're the only one to blame. Everyone will know it's your fault. I'll tell them that you were a shitty mother, about the way you didn't look after her, the way you were never there for us, let alone her, who is a young girl. I will tell everyone of the ways you failed us as a mother, and no one will forgive you."

The words still ring in my ear. All of it thought out in garbled English and yelled out in Spanish to my small, tired, middle-aged mother. My words bounced off the streets,

---

[20] Ibid.

reached the neighbors, and then disintegrated into the thickness of the dark. I was twenty, and I was learning that I had a powerful voice, a powerful thing I could use to mentally maim Mami and anyone who stood pressed or brushed my fragile ego.

"*No me culpes, hijo mío*," she responded to me calmly, without emotion.

Her words, even today, I refuse to translate. She felt in Spanish what I felt in English, and her pain was not like mine. She was Mami. I was her son. I tormented her with the fear I felt in my heart but refused to contain. I kept yelling into the night, and Mami eventually shed her tears of steel. I scratched my head and thought to myself, nothing good ever happens here. Julissa might make the headlines of the *New York Daily News*. The familiar journalist on Telemundo might run a story on this depending on how bad it is.

I should tell you that back then I did not sound like this, i.e., the way in which I am writing now. If I wanted to be accurate about how I said things, it would require too many contractions, slang, and made-up words in Spanglish and East New York English, which are sure to cloud up what I now feel and want to share. My language has changed. Brooklyn, too, has changed since I was a kid. East New York has even changed, or rather, I should say, it has been gentrified. Or, to put it simply, the white people with money have moved in. They've brought their degrees and dungarees and are *dique* developing without fear of the hood.[21]

When I finally decided to call the police, we were both tired of yelling, tired of the long, bitter shouting that

---

[21] Supposedly.

compelled the *chismosos* to carefully slide open their curtains or blinds, pressing their noses against their foggy windows.[22]

The cops never came for us. Moments later, a police car did slowly creep up the street to only stop in front of my neighbor's building to answer a different call. As the two policemen climbed up the steep steps of that building, my peripheral vision noticed the short and jolly steps of a familiar gait. It was Julissa, unaware of all that had happened, walking up Sunnyside to the angriest person in Brooklyn that December night. I felt my body convulse with a boiling *piqué*, reminding me of who I was, a small person who was raised angrily, fed anger, defecated anger.[23] I was about to unleash every bit of that on my block.

As soon as our eyes locked, Julissa knew I was burning with fury, that the next words to come out of my mouth were going to be scary, loud, painful. After yelling her name to make sure the darkness wasn't playing tricks on me, the five words I shouted after almost tore my vocal cords: "GET THE FUCK INSIDE NOW!" It was as if I collected every speck of rage I had inside me, the hate I planned to slowly give to Mami, into a mass of belligerent hostility. I was the center of it all; I was dark matter and whatever unknown thing was responsible for our existence, and I sunk deep into my oblivion.

Julissa's eyes did not prompt me. Tears flowed, almost instantly, following my words. They broke through her face, matching Mami's sobs. A union of fear and pain met on that stoop. Julissa brushed past me and ran inside the building. The cops, who were now descending my neighbor's stairs and

---

[22] Gossipmongers.

[23] Pique (but more intense).

looking toward me, seemed pleased to have something to do or someone to arrest.

"Were you the one who screamed?" one cop asked me. "What is the problem here?" he continued.

I don't remember answering them. Many more law enforcement questions followed. I just simply said that we were alright now, that she was now home as if they knew what I was talking about. The cops seemed to understand or were placated by Mami standing still near the building's iron gates. The policemen's car lights reflected oddly on my Mami's moist and wan face. The muted red and blue held me in my criminality, and for some reason, it didn't bother me. I was a criminal. I committed crimes against my family, against myself. Mami's God, I used to think, was watching, taking stock of all my offences. And I didn't care.

With Julissa safely inside and the cops moving on to the next block, I found myself outside, alone with Mami. The whirlwind of thoughts in my head didn't form words. The calm and relief of knowing Julissa was safe cleared my mind for just a moment. In that clarity, I saw it: another episode. I'd lost control of my temper, my body, my voice. This used to happen a lot, these sudden fits of rage that tore through me, leaving me feeling like some sort of fleshy empty vessel for a monster. For years, I numbed the aftermath, the guilt. I buried it deep. But as the anger drained from my chest, I knew I'd just torn Mami down with my words. This wasn't just about Julissa being missing. This was about me seeking some twisted form of vengeance, some sick catharsis through words or worse. It was an open invitation for my oldest, most familiar companion: my anger. The only emotion that ever made sense, the only one that captured just how hurt, confused, sad, and utterly forgotten I'd always felt. I sat on the stoop in silence, waiting for her to speak first, as my anger gently shut the door behind itself on the way out.

"*Esto fue lo último contigo. Me voy. No puedo vivir así. Hoy mismo, me voy.*"

This wasn't the first time she'd threatened to leave, and once again, I let the idea drift right over my head, landing in the spam folder of my mind. I puffed out my chest, blurting the first thing that came to mind. "Go! Don't nobody need you." But deep down, I was crumbling. I was terrified, out of school, broke, working a dead-end job. I played the tough guy, but the thought of Mami leaving me to fend for myself? It horrified me. She wouldn't really leave, would she? She knew I couldn't pay the rent without her, couldn't even keep myself fed. Hell, I couldn't even do my own laundry. I didn't know how to work those ancient machines next to the bodega. How many quarters did they take? Where do you even put the detergent? What even is detergent?

Mami wasn't bluffing this time. Everyone has a breaking point, and she had finally reached hers. She marched into the apartment and started packing. This was home. I made my first real friends in this place, felt lucky to have a mother who cooked for us. These walls watched me grow from a kid to a teenager to whatever it is I am now. But none of that mattered at this moment. I knew I had screwed up in ways I couldn't even put into words, but my budding *machismo* held them back, sealed tight.

Mami was leaving me—retracing the same steps Papi took when he walked out on us. She packed a small bag for her and Julissa. Both were crying, holding hands, moving in silence, as if speaking would make it all too real. Then they left. The door clicked shut behind them. I just sat there, heart pounding, eyes fixed on the knob, frozen on the stoop.

Maybe this wasn't what you expected when you picked up this book. Maybe you weren't looking for the memoirs of an angry Brooklyn twenty-year old with a serious anger-management problem. But what *did* you expect?

When we see, read, or hear the word *Dominican*—on TV, in headlines, in academic studies—we get the same tired script: racial denial, anti-blackness, sandy beaches and cheap-ass rum, loose women, hypersexual men.

"Dominicans don't like the color of their skin."

"Dominicans hate Haitians."

"Dominican men are *mujeriegos*—kids all over the place."[24]

" They can play baseball but beat their women."

"Every Dominican got a little Trujillo in them, clawing out behind the ears."

These are the stories that stick. These are the stories that drown the details of our existence. And yes, our history as a people—as a nation—is built on colonialism, slavery, and white supremacy. That's a fact. The pages that follow won't counter that.

But we're also angry twenty-year-old boys living in Brooklyn, trying to be human in a world that treats us like we don't belong.

---

[24] Womanizer and playboy.

2

Until I am free to write bilingually and to switch codes without having always to translate, while I still have to speak English or Spanish when I would rather speak Spanglish, and as long as I have to accommodate the English speakers rather than having them accommodate me, my tongue will be illegitimate. I will no longer be made to feel ashamed of existing. I will have my voice.

Gloria Anzaldúa[25]

The day after Mami left, I woke up like nothing had happened—at least until reality crashed in, a lead weight on my chest. The absence of Mami's safety net pressed down on me, pinning me to the bed, eyes fixed on the ceiling. The life ahead unfurled in my mind, and suddenly, all those things my high school teachers droned on about "the real world" started to make sense. Tough, cold, unforgiving. Their warnings pounded through my head, an unwelcome soundtrack to my spiraling thoughts.

Lost in this mental fog, Gabriel wandered into my room. I'm two years older than him, but growing up, those years felt like a whole lifetime. It's funny how things flip; sometimes I look at him now and see an older brother. He's always been more carefree than me, and I've always envied that. When I

---

[25] Gloria Anzaldúa, *Borderlands: La Frontera: The New Mestiza* (1987).

told him everything that went down the night before, he didn't even flinch.

He immediately started talking about the perks of living on our own: the girls he could bring over to show off his new "adult responsibilities." At that moment, we were completely clueless. We had no idea how to make rent, do laundry, pay bills, cook, or even just fend for ourselves. But there he was, already dreaming up our new life, blissfully unaware of the storm we were walking into.

Thanks to Mami, dinner had always been free and delicious. We come from a very traditional Dominican family, not Dominican like the friars who followed Saint Dominic, but Dominican like the ones who were oppressed and killed by Trujillo for being too dark or for butchering the Spanish language. Dominicans like the ones you might have heard about up in Washington Heights, running the corner bodegas. Like many families from our homeland, we came to this country with the same hopes and dreams as any immigrant, chasing things we never had, yearning for comforts I probably take for granted now: electricity, hot water, dollars, health insurance, food. I was just a kid when we arrived. It was winter, and it was the first time I had ever seen snow. But that's another story.

Gabriel was with me through those early months of our uncertain independence, trying to lift my spirits, always talking about the next dish he wanted to learn. Cooking was a necessity. Eating out was a luxury we couldn't afford. But he threw himself into it and eventually became a decent chef, at least by my standards. He even landed a job as a cook and delivery boy at a small deli with a view of the 59th Street Bridge. Or, as people in Queens know it, the Queensboro

Bridge, now officially the Ed Koch Bridge. F. Scott Fitzgerald immortalized that bridge in *The Great Gatsby* when Nick Carraway said, "the city seen from the Queensboro Bridge is always the city seen for the first time, in its first wild promise of all the mystery and all the beauty in the world." But Gabriel and I? We didn't feel that way. The Queensboro Bridge brought to mind Nas and Mobb Deep, *Illmatic* and "Shook Ones," and Queensbridge Houses.

Gabriel worked long hours, Monday through Friday, sometimes even on weekends to make a little extra cash. His dream of becoming an independent adult was finally happening, while I was still holding on, waiting for Mami to return and forgive me for what I had done.

I kept grinding away at my dead-end job, full-time on a Tropicana juice delivery route—just like Papi used to do. He had graduated to driving a cab, so it was just me now: the helper and the driver, sweating through the streets like we owed somebody something.

If you've never done this kind of work, you can't really understand how grueling it is. Papi made it look easy. Then again, he only brought me along a handful of times in the sixteen years he lived with us. Maybe he was protecting me. Or maybe he knew this kind of job—the kind that breaks your back and eats your soul—ain't the kind you pass down, even if it's the only thing you got to offer.

He was in the cash business. I doubt he ever got a paycheck like the ones they handed us at the end of the week. And even those—checks with your name on them—felt more like a joke. Something official for a job that left you feeling disposable. Checks are for people with on-the-books jobs. But those of us off the books, we dealt in sweat and silence. Papi's closest version of a paycheck was a traffic ticket.

Tropicana paid in cash. Only cash. And it felt like a bribe. That job taught me things no school ever could. It taught me that the body can fail you. That even when your fingers lock up and your lower back screams, you still have to will yourself to bend, to lift, to push that hand truck stacked with 300 pounds of juice boxes down into some rat-infested cellar that smelled like mildew and spoiled produce.

By mid-afternoon, under the summer sun, my skin was hot to the touch, brown and burning from exposure. I could smell myself: not just the sweat, but the faint crackle of fried skin cells flaking off my arms. My shirt stuck to my back, my socks were soaked, and still I had hours to go.

And all around me, windows and sidewalks and rooftop patios, I saw people sheltered. Folks behind air-conditioned glass, sipping something cold, scrolling through something meaningless. People whose hands weren't calloused, who didn't have to clench with all their might just to hold on to their rent money. I envied them. I envied anyone with a space heater, a fan, a job that didn't grind you down to nothing.

But that job also taught me something else. Something I wasn't ready to say out loud for a long time: my time was worth more than what they were paying me. My mind—my imagination, my stories, my thoughts—was mine. No boss could take that unless I gave it away.

So yeah, it was an education. In shame. In exhaustion. In what it means to give your body to work that doesn't love you back. But it was also a lesson in resistance. Because even when the job tried to strip me of worth, I knew deep down: they could never afford my mind. With my job at Tropicana, I managed to scrape together my half of the rent, five hundred dollars. For New York City, that's practically unheard of, but we had luck on our side. The apartment was rent-controlled, so legally the building's owners couldn't charge us more than we could afford. But even then, that five hundred felt nearly impossible to come up with. Gabriel covered the other half, and for the first few months, we made it work. We were happy, or at least content, until we realized that working just to pay rent wasn't much of a life. It wasn't the kind of life either of us wanted.

We tried to maintain some semblance of a life outside of work. Gabriel was way better at it than I was. He'd hit the basketball courts at a nearby park whenever he had the chance, keeping himself in good shape. But music was his real passion. He had a knack for it, switching between Spanish and English in his raps with ease, sometimes blending both languages in a single track. His only vice was cigarettes. He loved to smoke, whether it was a bogie every few hours or a blunt to unwind after work.

I never picked up the habit. Weed only made my problems feel more real, like a cop or an eviction notice breathing down my neck. I was too paranoid to indulge. Always worried the building's management would find out Mami wasn't living with us anymore. The lease was in her name, and the threat of eviction was a constant shadow. That fear clung to me, even now, always whispering that we were one step away from losing everything.

I lived in a constant state of anxiety and fear, trapped in an unknowingness toward life. My shortsighted perception of the world left room for only one thought: immediate survival.

Future worries felt like a luxury, completely irrelevant to my current reality. This was the beginning of my so-called independent adulthood.

Five months after Mami and Julissa left, Gabriel and I sat down to talk about our economic mess.

"Man," Gabriel sighed, "what are we going to do about this rent, about this apartment? I have no money for myself, none to take girls out. We have to figure something out." He cracked open a Dutchmaster, spilling the guts into a black plastic bag. "Tell me, what should we do? It was your fault they left."

He never got tired of throwing that moment in my face, making it my burden. As if every bad thing that happened to him since then was entirely my fault. In his eyes, I was responsible for everything—the crimes in Brownsville, the hunger in small Dominican and Haitian towns, the war in Southwest Asia. I carried that weight on my shoulders, crushed under the blame he piled on me.

"You're acting like all of this is only my fault. Let's think of ways of making more money, of working less hours and doing other things with our lives," I responded.

"Like what?"

He grunted as he crushed the kush with his nails over a past due rent statement.

"What the *FUCK* do you suggest we do?" he said with a sly, paradoxical smile.

Gabriel was always giddy before lighting up a blunt packed with what he called "the best weed East New York had to offer."

My brother was a straight-up marijuana connoisseur. If there were such a thing as a Ph.D. in Weed Studies, he'd be tenured. He could tell you exactly what strain you were smoking—whether it was Sour Diesel, Blue Dream, OG Kush, or something new off the block. He knew how to smoke it right too: in a bong, a Dutch Master, a Philly, a roll-up paper, or just straight raw leaf. He even knew which dealer had what, who sold grams or eighths, who taxed, and who gave a little extra if you were cool.

Weed lifted him. Took him off the sticky floors of our messy apartment and into a state of proper I-don't-give-a-fuck-ness.

Back then, I had no real dreams or aspirations. I just wanted to make the rent and skateboard every day for the rest of my life. I guess the closest thing to a passion I had was skateboarding. The wood on wheels got me through the roughest times. It got me through Mami's departure. There is something about the way the ground feels underneath me when the toughness of the street is made soft by four wheels on a fresh deck. It is a unique way to feel the earth. The skateboard translates the language of the streets and sidewalks into a vibration that rattles from the heels of your feet to every part of your body, brain included. You feel your muscles working as you maintain balance. Your brain shuts down, and everything becomes simple. The world becomes clearer; you might notice how the wind blows, how the sun shines, how the ground smooths underneath your feet. I skated through Brooklyn when I had nothing else to do and reflected on the changing landscape and faces before me.

Sunnyside wasn't in the safest neighborhood, but it wasn't the most dangerous either. It was my block, my stoop, the one place where time stood still.

One day coming home from the juice route, I skated through Bedford Stuyvesant to get home and realized how much had changed. Due to the unyielding power of "development," you'll hear some people call *Do, or Die Bed-Stuy*, "Stuyvesant Heights." I can only assume that those who decide the naming of these places associate "Heights" with progress and white people similar to the way some of my friends and colleagues think of Prospect Heights and Brooklyn Heights. Back then, "Heights," for me, heightened nothing at all. I associated the word with other places, places I feared and avoided growing up, including Crown Heights and Washington Heights.

I still believe my fears were justified. As a young immigrant teenager, such places introduced me to incomprehensible violence. I was subject to a type of fear that can only be felt in the mind. It was a panic constructed from different external sources: poverty, race, and language, which tainted a lot of what I remember about my childhood, even though I know there must have been happy moments. It was this system of reality that kept returning me to my high school days, when the world was too taut to give me anything other than a sigh.

Three years passed before Mami and I spoke again. At first, it was just stubbornness and anger that kept us apart, but eventually, it turned into habit—then shame—and finally, fear. Julissa grew into a teenager during that time, navigating the rough transition without her older brother around. I knew that must've been hard on her, and I wasn't there.

Mami leaving was the best thing that could've happened to me, even though those years without her were filled with financial and psychological struggles. I hated who I had become: angry, afraid, and entitled, obsessed with being respected in the hood and what people thought of me. When she left, she took all the things that reminded me of what I had become. I had a chance to start over, free from the weight of my past mistakes.

With her, she took the Dominican poverty I was ashamed of: the food stamps that made me feel eternally impoverished, the crosses and santos I had stopped talking to, and the rules that felt like they were molding me into someone who was barely surviving.

When Mami left, the apartment walls were blank, and I filled them with my own dreams. A life-size poster of Jimi Hendrix wailing on the guitar, a world map that made me feel less confined, bookshelves stacked with books I found on the street or that friends gave me. These things became the repertoire of my new life, symbols of the person I was trying to become.

I think most of us reach a point when we crave distance from our parents or caregivers, the very people who have shaped us. There's something about that distance, that space to be without them, that lets us discover and nurture a new version of ourselves. That's what Mami's departure did for me. It opened the door to a blank room, where I found a mirror—and eventually, I learned to look at the reflection I saw.

3

Buscando visa para un sueño.

Juan Luis Guerra[26]

In my days at Boys and Girls High School (or "the High" as we called it), I read the sidewalks and walls around our school like poetry. Every crack and scribble felt like a symbol, an objective correlative to what I felt in my heart. I remember the grayness, the shadows that filled those halls. I even dressed the part: gray t-shirt, gray and white Jordan 12s, gray New Era 76ers hat. Gray was my favorite color because it was all I saw: the sky, the brick buildings, the sidewalks, and, somehow, me.

My gray days started early, at 6:00 a.m. sharp. Mami made sure Gabriel and I were up and ready for school. We went to different high schools. My parents didn't understand the New York City high school admissions process, so they had us pick schools on a whim. I chose Boys and Girls mainly because of its name; it sounded like a nice, safe place. Gabriel picked a school his junior high friends were going to, which made more sense. I was in Bed Stuy and he was in the Rockaways, at a school called Beach Channel High School.

---

[26] Juan Luis Guerra, "Visa para un Sueño," *Ojalá Que Llueva Café* (1989).

Beach Channel had a reputation for high dropout and teenage pregnancy rates. Gabriel eventually dropped out, but to his credit, he didn't get anyone pregnant. So, he only half-lived up to the school's rep.

His school was an hour away by train, while mine was just ten minutes. Yet, even with just one stop on the A train, I could never seem to make it to school on time.

I didn't know it then, but I was lucky during my time at the High. The school's principal was Dr. Frank Mickens, a legendary Brooklyn educator and no-nonsense visionary who transformed Boys and Girls High School from one of the most underperforming and dangerous schools in the country into what he called "the pride and joy of Bed-Stuy."

Mick, as we called him, wasn't just some outsider with a clipboard and a plan. He was from the neighborhood. He grew up in a tenement building not far from the school and was himself an alumnus of Boys High, back when it was still all-boys and still one of the few avenues out for working-class Black youth in Brooklyn. Like many of the young men who walked through those halls—myself included—he played basketball and even coached the team early in his career before moving into administration.

Mick was loud, commanding, and often unorthodox. He implemented what many at the time saw as radical policies: a strict no-jewelry rule, mandatory shirts and ties every Monday and Tuesday, and an unrelenting emphasis on discipline and pride. That's actually how I learned to tie a tie— because of *him*. Four years of pressed shirts and stiff collars, even though my own father never wore one to work. But of course, we found ways to add our own Brooklyn flair. We'd throw a jersey over the button-up or rock a Coogi sweater on top. It was a look that only made sense at the High.

By the time I got there, Mick wasn't jogging up and down the hallways like he used to—catching kids coming in late or barking at them to tuck in their shirts. But his presence was still felt. I remember him sometimes just sitting in a chair in the middle of the hallway when the bell rang, watching the wave of students rush to class like a general surveying his troops. He'd often have a crate filled with snacks—fruit snacks, a honey bun, a juice box. Little things, but meaningful coming from him.

I was afraid of Mick—of his disciplinarian reputation. One day, I was running late to class, and he stopped me. We were alone in the hallway, and I thought I was dead meat. But he didn't yell. He barely batted an eye. He just called to me in a rare soft voice, "Young man, why aren't you in class?"

I nervously apologized, my accents spilling out of my mouth. "I'm sorry—the train…" We always blamed the train. "The train was slow."

"Being on time means being early, young man. And being early is how you get ahead."

Those weren't his exact words. It was something just as baffling and profound. My heart was pounding, and then he just sent me on my way.

Mick retired in 2004, not long after I graduated, and passed away in 2009. But the standard he set, the energy he brought, and the sense of belonging he helped cultivate—those stayed with the High long after he was gone.

Boys and Girls High is a zoned school right in the heart of Bed-Stuy. This was the early 2000s, before the wave of hipsters crashed onto Brooklyn's shores. The student body was ninety-seven percent Black, with the rest mostly Latine, or Hispanic, as it was commonly said back then. Being one of the few immigrant Hispanics, I stood out. I was different, and I was ashamed of it, ashamed of my first tongue, my hair, my skin color, even my name, which sounded to many like some mysterious dish with too many spices.

Not a day went by that I didn't fantasize about flying away, past the gray clouds, back to the Dominican Republic where it was warm, where people spoke and looked like me.

Once I passed through my school's metal detectors, among the first ever used in any U.S. high school, I walked to my first class. Everything was a dull blur, much like the gray sky, buildings, sheets of paper, and fog that surrounded me. I don't remember learning much. I was too anxious to let my guard down, too focused on fitting in. Learning wasn't a priority when I was trying to avoid getting jumped by the Bloods, Crips, or anyone who looked at me with silent distrust. The latter were the more volatile ones.

At the High, it felt like we were constantly proving ourselves to each other, which limited our potential and, tragically, sometimes even led to death. Now, I think I understand the roots of that violence: societal rejection, poverty, racism, and a popular culture that binds young Black and Brown teens to the hood. Back then, though, none of this made sense to me.

There's a day that lives rent-free in my mind. It sums up my entire high school experience. I was sixteen and got into the only fight I ever had there. It was a fair fight, and I won. That made me look tough, like a G, and people either loved or hated me for it. Of course, that meant the other guy was humiliated, broken, and ridiculed.

Believe it or not, it was Nathaniel Hawthorne who started the fight that day. His *Scarlet Letter* threw me into a mess I didn't see coming. It all started during fifth period English with Mrs. Simone, who assigned the 1994 Dover Thrift Edition. The cover stood out immediately—bold, with that iconic red letter "A" splashed across a black background. I thought the book was pretty cool, especially since my name starts with an "A" and red's my favorite color. Plus, the book's about an adulteress. I remember thinking, "Yes! This sounds spicy." *The Scarlet Letter* was one of the only two books I actually read in high school, the other being J.D. Salinger's *The Catcher in the Rye*.

Vernon, who everyone called Vern, sat right behind me in Mrs. Simone's class. We were kind of friends. One day, during our class discussion on the novel, Mrs. Simone asked for our general thoughts. I raised my hand and said something about how the book must've been pretty scandalous when it was first published. I added, "I'm actually liking it."

Apparently, that was more than Vern could handle. He let out this loud grunt, forcing me to turn and face him. I knew my nerdy comments could open me up to ridicule, but I didn't think anyone cared enough to react. Turns out, I was wrong.

"Yo! You on that book's dick, son!" Vern shouted from behind me, dragging out the word *dick* just enough to send everyone—except me—into a fit of laughter.

Mrs. Simone looked quizzically at Vern then at me, wondering, I'm sure, what "on that book's dick?" even meant. She told Vern to shut up. I felt the pores on my face open, body temperature rising, my teeth clenching. I knew exactly what he meant through his nonsensical metaphor. Everyone knew what he meant. Being on the *Scarlet Letter*'s proverbial dick was a homophobic dig. It meant that I was riding it, sucking up to it, and thus sucking up to the teacher, being smart, sucking something else no doubt (Hawthorne's meat, who knows?) being all the things that could get you jumped or even killed. And for that reason, I was beyond offended. His remark reminded me of the straight-A student I had been in bilingual junior high and elementary school, how I gave up being a good student in high school to fit in, and how I thought I would never be able to be smart again. Vern's words reminded me that I was no longer capable of academic excellence. I didn't have awards or certificates to give to Mami, who loved showing them off to the *vecinas*.[27]

I looked at Vern straight in his pupils and said, "Yo, Vern, after school, you and me, Imma fuck you up!" His eyes showed a slight sign of distress. I was serious, and he knew it, but he couldn't show it, not in front of the whole class after that display. Mrs. Simone told us both to shut up or leave the classroom. We both kept our mouths shut for the rest of the class period.

After school, I walked down the Utica train station with my boy, Antoine, one of the most laid-back guys I knew. Antoine tried talking me out of the fight.

"Are you really going to fight him because of what he said about that book?"

---

[27] Neighbors.

"It's not just the book, Antoine. He thinks he's tough. And he disrespected. I'm not letting that slide."

Once we went through the turnstile and down the stairs, I spotted Vern leaning on one of the station posts with his arms crossed, clocking my every step. We locked eyes.

"Yo, chill," said Antoine.

"Nah, fuck that. Look at him, he thinks he's tough," I said, loud enough for Vern to hear me. I took off my ENYCE jacket as I walked up to Vern and punched him two or three times in his face.

Vern did not retaliate. He just stood there, eating my punches, saying "Your punches ain't shit; you hit like a girl."

The speeding A train interrupted this pathetic scene. I looked at Vern as he wiped his face. I told him not to board this train. Antoine and I got on. Vern stayed behind, likely planning his vengeance. I had no idea what this Hawthorne beef had in store for me. No one wins if the fight never ends.

4

Be having dreams that I'm a gangsta, drinking Moets, holding TECs
Making sure the cash came correct, then I stepped . . .

Nas[28]

The next day, thirty kids dressed in their finest, brightest blue waited for me after school on the Utica train station. The A and C trains sped by but students refused to get on. There was a fight to be seen. Empty train cars zoomed past the congested station. Everyone on the platform was talking about it. And everyone wanted a piece of me. People knew me in high school because I stood out for what I *wasn't*. To most of my classmates, I was the "Spanish boy with the ponytail." Yeah, I had a ponytail. *Fuck you!*

"The Spanish boy with the ponytail is going to get jumped by all these Crips. Is he Blood?"

As I walked down the platform steps, I heard their voices, their laughter, and I knew without looking into their faces, into their eyes, that they were laughing at me. The steel I felt in my throat kept me on my toes as I descended the train station steps. As my classmates gossiped about the number of

---

[28] Nas, "N.Y. State of Mind," *Illmatic* (1994).

Crips waiting for me, I walked to what I was sure would be my death. But I was like Gabriel then, and my ego walked me coolly toward the noise, alongside two of my boys, Carlos and Anthony. We took the train together every day. I grew up with Carlos, a brilliant kid and talented athlete. If it weren't for him, I probably would have dropped out of high school. He was enthusiastic about learning, so having him around for my junior and senior years motivated me to graduate. Anthony was my best friend in high school. He was a tall Panamanian kid, one of the few in the school who spoke better Spanish than me, bright, and humble, which was a rare thing at Boys and Girls. All the tall kids were on the basketball team; and since we had one of the best teams in the city, the players felt better than the rest of the student body. Anthony sucked at ball, which explained his humility. As the three of us walked down the steps to the train, Carlos and Anthony probably knew that I was dead meat, but they were braver than me.

"There he is," someone murmured.

"It's goin' down," another person said, faceless commentators everywhere. The group that had come for me looked toward me but not at me. They did not know who I was. Their target could have been any one of us. Then someone said, "The Spanish boy with the long hair," and I was quickly identified. My pride kicked in.

"What's good!" I said. At the center of the group stood someone who looked like the leader. He looked tougher than the rest, more experienced. Smirking, he walked up to me with his white and blue Jordan Sixers leading him, one step at a time. This was the era of retro Jordans and throwback jerseys. We all looked like we played for different basketball teams, like an All-Star game.

Surrounding us, the Utica Avenue station's red and black tiled walls contrasted with the different shades of blue sported by these teenagers and young adults. The rest of us wore black North Faces and throwback jerseys. We were a technicolor bunch but too dangerous to stare at.

I noticed the leader's Jordans because I had them on too.

"What's good, son," he said, sounding like DMX. "I heard you tried to jump my son Vern, duke."

In junior high school, this introductory spiel would have never happened. These guys would have jumped me on sight—*no need to talk to the chubby Dominican boy with a pushback. He is a punk and talk is cheap, dead meat.* In my senior year of high school, people considered me tough because I dressed like I sold drugs and talked like I had been raised in the streets, or at least I thought I did. I wasn't afraid to speak my mind and played it as cool as the next troubled, impoverished, and unsettled minority.

"What's good," I replied. "Ain't nobody jump your boy. It was a fair fight, and he lost."

The leader looked at Vern and then back at me, and suddenly, everyone seemed to be looking only at me. I thought back to my junior high years. The only reason I looked and talked the way I did now was because I had to. Junior high hadn't prepared me for Boys and Girls High School. I'm not just talking about academics. I'm talking about ass-whooping, life-saving preparation.

In middle school, my bilingual teachers were both mentors and protectors. They were links to my birth tongue and my culture. In those classrooms, I was shielded from the ridicule of my English accent, from my *Dominicanidad*. Us bilingual kids were all from somewhere else, and in that way, we felt tied to each other. But when, in seventh grade, I graduated to all-English classes, it felt like I was being forced out of that safe room. Speaking English wasn't enough, and I knew it. Not to survive. To do that, I had to fit in, and isn't that the story of every teenager. The question: How do I fit in because fitting in is about survival?

You do not become gangsta-like overnight. It takes years, many fights, a lot of clothes, a little swag, the right connections, a reputation, and most importantly, respect. For me, being a *dique* gangsta was like writing. You get better at it, but only slightly and if you don't come from a tradition of it, you must work that much harder to embody it.

Up until high school, I was, to most of the people who met me and myself, a punk-ass Dominican immigrant. I was kept in a tight bilingual bubble for the first years of grammar school. It was when they pushed me out of it that I realized I would not make it far without a harder shell. I thought learning English would be enough to assimilate and be successful (and that is truer if you're an adult and don't have to be in school with thousands of others who think very little of "your punk Spanish ass"). After learning to speak in English, I had to unlearn it and learn hood English. Hood English, however, is ever-changing: and to be fluent means to keep up with hood culture. I learned it fairly well and was able to mute the sounds of the punk ass Spanish kid inside of me.

"Y'all goin' to fight the fair one now." The leader said.

He scratched his cornrow and told his group to make room. A circular ring walled by throwback jerseys and hundred dollar shoes barricaded Vern and me. I quickly took off my North Face jacket, the Hyvent edition with that secret side pocket. I handed it to Anthony. Under it, I had on an L.A. Clippers warmup jersey four times my size. I handed it to Carlos. I was left in a blue shirt, which I thought was ironic then without knowing the word for it, since most of Vern's friends were Crips. I rolled up my blue Harlem tee on the sleeves, showing off my newly developed muscles in hope of intimidating Vern, who had thirty Crips with him to intimidate me. I apparently looked like the bully in this situation, for a woman, maybe in her twenties broke through the crowd and grabbed Vern as she yelled,

"Y'all going to leave him alone. Ain't none of this going down here," the stranger said, pulling Vern away from me.

If she only knew that I was the one who was in trouble, that all of these Crips were after me and wanted me on the floor, jerseyless, North Faceless, and Jordanless, maybe in the tracks.

"Y'all better get out of here. Y'all not goin' to bully this poor kid," the woman continued.

Students and bystanders bursted into laughter. Some sighed in disappointment. I grinned, a mix of relief and pride washing over me. Whether she meant to or not, that woman had just saved my ass. The second I threw that first punch, I knew I was in for a beating, one that could've left me unrecognizable. I've seen smaller crews turn athletes into patients. But Vern's boys were different, disorganized, thrown off balance.

The woman who stepped in pulled Vern away, and suddenly, the chaos paused. Everyone looked confused. I knew it was my chance to slip away. Carlos handed me my warmup jersey, and Anthony passed me my coat. We could hear the screech of the approaching train, like a safety whistle calling me home. All I had to do was get on it.

The doors slid open. Without a word or a glance back at the pack, the three of us stepped onto the train. I thought we were in the clear, but no. They saw us. They couldn't let it end like that. One by one, they piled in behind us. Vern was fuming, humiliated in front of his crew, in front of everyone at school. He couldn't just let it go.

They crammed into my car, their eyes locked on me. Vern, trying to save face, so the leader strode up and asked, "Where you getting off?"

I didn't flinch. "Broadway Junction," I replied.

He said, "Aight, that's where we'll do this then."

As the leader walked away, I turned to Anthony and Carlos and said, "This isn't over. Vern and his crew will follow me all the way home if they have to."

Broadway Junction was only two stops away from the High on the C train, but We'd taken the express A, cutting the time in half. When the conductor called out the stop and the doors slid open, we stepped onto the platform, slowly. Running wasn't an option. Our pride wouldn't let us, and besides, they didn't want a chaotic chase. No, they wanted to jump me the right way, like some twisted initiation, except there'd be no flag or secret handshake waiting for me at the end.

Broadway Junction, with its bright blue-tiled walls, seemed to reflect the wave of Crips surging behind us. Some of them clearly lived nearby, picking up more members as they marched up the platform, swelling their ranks. Some wore blue; others, faces flushed with anger and tension, were ready to explode. They moved like a violent river after a storm, gathering strength and force with every step. I felt like I was about to drown in that flood.

At least this beating wouldn't happen in front of the entire school, I thought. Small consolation. Who was I kidding? If I made it out alive, my swollen face and battered body would tell the story anyway. My classmates would know exactly what had gone down.

We kept moving, slow and deliberate, with Vern's crew trailing us like predators. The leader caught up, walking beside me, and again asked where I wanted this fight to go down. I just wanted to get home, so I told him, "We'll take the J train to Van Siclen. That's where Carlos and I live."

Broadway Junction allows mass commuters to select services from four trains (A, C, L, and J). I always took the J home even though I could easily walk it home from there. The J train was less crowded, and if it wasn't for the elderly woman and the two construction workers spread unevenly throughout the cart, we would have been alone with Vern's crew.

"This is Van Siclen Avenue," said the static voice from the PA system, and the doors opened.

Out we all came, walking in unison toward the steps. *It's all over now*, I thought to myself. *There is no way this endless search for a battlefield will continue any longer.* The group walked down the stairs with us, moving closer to us now. Van Siclen Station used to have a large mezzanine level outside which was used as the waiting area, thirty feet above the street, and the spot where it would all go down. We all stood on that balcony, with a view of the corner pizzeria and corner bodega. One of them, the biggest one of the group who I recognized as the linebacker of my school's football team, blocked the doors with his imposing size.

"Aight, this is it. Y'all ready?" the leader asked.

I said nothing. Carlos and Anthony looked how I imagined *I* looked, terrified but paralyzed. Inaudible talk and laughter ensued around us. I thought of my family and the way they were going to react if these boys beat me to death, or if I survived and got home looking like I was in a bad car accident.

The leader smiled and asked me, "You scared?" and touched my heart. He felt my fear. "Yeah. You scared. Aight, let's do this," he said, and again, as if rehearsed, they circled us.

The wall of colors and sneakers closed in on us, and time stopped.

"YO CARLOS, IS THAT YOU, SON?" someone suddenly yelled from the street.

"O hell fuckin no! Y'all mother fuckers ain't jumpin' no one," cried Sheeka, a Panamánien much older than us.

Sheeka noticed the crowd from the corner pizzeria. And seeing that the strangers surrounded us, he came to the rescue. Sheeka was cool with everyone in the hood and sometimes even played pickup games with us at the park.

"Grab the *Hammer,* Cito," he yelled to a local G standing next to him, who everyone knew not to fuck with.

My alleged attackers were as alarmed as we were relieved. And like roaches under the unexpected gleam of a 2:00 am light bulb, they dispersed. Carlos, Anthony, and I were left there with our thoughts.

I'll never forget that, Sheeka, my hero, thank you.

Walking through the halls the next day, I couldn't shake the feeling of unease. It was as if the incident could replay itself at any moment. I avoided eye contact with everyone except my closest friends. To distract myself, I'd stare blankly at the list of notable alumni on the walls, wondering what happened to the promise those names once gave to our school. Isaac Asimov, Shirley Chisholm, Norman Mailer, Man Ray, graduates of the oldest public high school in Brooklyn. Yet, to my younger, more naïve eyes, the only promise our school seemed to offer was through the men's basketball team, the Kangaroos. coached by the legendary Ruth Lovelace. "Coach Love," as everyone called her, in my eyes, was the most impressive and intimidating person to walk those hallways.

Coach Ruth Lovelace's inspiration for basketball must've started at home. Her father, a former track and field star for the Boys and Girls Kangaroos, laid the foundation. She followed in his footsteps, first as a standout player on the Girls' team basketball team, where she broke scoring records and became a local legend in Bed-Stuy. Her dominance on the court wasn't just about points; it was about presence.

After graduating from Boys and Girls High, she earned a scholarship to Seton Hall University, where she made an immediate impact. During her time with the Pirates in the early '90s, a golden age for women's college basketball, she averaged 14 points and 3 assists per game. These were the years when women's basketball was gaining national attention, helped along by players like Ruth Lovelace, who played with grit and purpose before NIL deals and televised tournaments were the norm.

But her story didn't end there. After a series of injuries, she returned to Boys and Girls as a gym teacher. Shortly after, she was assigned by Principal Frank Mickens not to coach the girls' team, but the boys'. That year, she made history as the first woman in New York State to coach a boys' varsity high school basketball team, and one of the first in the entire country to do so.

Many were congratulatory about her position as coach, but there were always haters who believed that she, a woman, could never coach the Kangaroos, 10-time city champions and the "Pride and Joy of Bed-Stuy." She proved them all wrong. Under her leadership, she led the Kangaroos to multiple PSAL championships, producing top-tier college prospects.

Much of this is chronicled in the ESPN documentary *A Woman Among Boys* (2008), directed by Jon Alpert and Matthew O'Neill. It tells the story of Coach Love's leadership, her ability to turn around young men's lives through basketball, and her refusal to let anyone lower the bar academically or athletically.

But here's what a documentary won't tell you: Coach Love had mad swag. At 5'10", she could command a gym with just her walk. She was always rocking something fresh, whether it was a velour tracksuit or the latest Jordans. I still remember her patent leather 12s and the olive green 9s. But her swag wasn't just in her kicks or her fit. It was in her demeanor. She was soft-spoken but direct. Cool, but never passive. Caring, but never indulgent. You knew she expected more from you because she believed in you. She had this aura around, at least for me, that reminded you that you were among greatness.

In large part, that's why I wanted so badly to be on that team, not just to play, but to learn from her. Coach Love didn't just build players. She built men.

My junior year, I tried out for the team. I had been playing street basketball since the sixth grade, so I thought I'd sail through tryouts. At practice, Coach Love had us running laps around the gym, finishing each round with jumping jacks. My heart pounded, sweat trickled down my spine. I quickly realized street ball was nothing like organized basketball.

James, the point guard, glanced at me and asked if I was okay. I nodded, pushing through, but I didn't come back the next day. I quit before I even started and in enters one of my biggest high school regrets.

Street basketball became the only place I felt like I belonged, playing with people I knew, my boys. Unlike at school, where I drifted through the gray halls, wordless and alone. So, instead of going straight home after school, I'd head to Highland Park near my house and hooped until the street poles buzzed and burned with yellow glow.

Let me tell you a story about one of those days.

5

There's a war goin' on outside no man is safe from (Word?).
It don't matter if you three feet or eight-one (One).

Cam'ron[29]

We gathered around his fallen-hard body, his fingers coiling at the joints. He moved in and out of consciousness, his breath skipping seconds. Piss and blood poured out of him, mixing on the jagged concrete. It was his mortal aura, the body halo that led him to the world of the non-flesh. He was gunned down in front of a five-on-five full court game. His bike leaned on a Brooklyn-park bench. A faded Spalding ball bounced off the court and rolled under the jungle gyms. Cars in the distance zoomed pass, lifting a black plastic bag off the avenue. A pigeon glided over the park fence, and no one knew what to do.

"Do we lift him?" said one of the players, "Put him on the bench?"

"Don't fucking touch him!" shouted the dying boy's big bro.

---

[29] Cam'ron, "Welcome to New York City," *Come Home with Me* (2002).

70

For many of us there, our childhoods died the night Larry Hill Jr., the fifteen-year-old basketball player from Springfield Gardens, Queens, was killed. It was the summer of 2004, Lebron James's second season with the Cavs, Michael Jordan's first year in retirement after playing his final NBA game with the Washington Wizards. But we were living in the generation of the handlers. So, we didn't talk much about the Kid from Akron or Old MJ. To us Brooklyn boys, Akron was a foreign country that no trains could reach. And MJ was washed up. Our eyes were set on the dribblers of our time: Allen Iverson, God Shammgod, Stephon Marbury, Hot Sauce, and all the park legends, who despite being ball hogs, made us believe that the only thing to live for was the cross over. And for that reason, I spent the entire summer studying AND1 Mixtapes in hopes of finessing my handles.

Larry only had fifteen summers. For most of those summers, he was a little kid, without language, without permission to go outside. Most of those summers were supervised, steadied by parental hands, watched closely by his big bro. He probably had two or three good summers to be outside, by himself, to go to the park, and get a taste of grown-up freedom. Larry's dad, Larry Sr. would later tell a *New York Times* reporter that they moved their sons out of Springfield for a better life. Many Brooklyn cats have this stereotypical image of Queens as some safe distant suburb where only the rich live. But don't get it twisted. Queens has its wild parts. The frequent shootouts, killings, and robberies in Springfield were enough for any family with the means to leave to get up and go.

"It really hurts," Larry's dad said, "because I thought I was moving into a real quiet neighborhood. I thought my kids were safe."[30]

The two bullets that pierced Larry's slender back interrupted his transition from youth to adulthood. I watched Larry's eyes fill with shock, wondering if he knew he was dying. When you're a teenager, death seems far away, like something that can't, and perhaps won't ever, touch you. But death was right in front of us that night. It was doing Larry's breathing for him, his seeing. Larry looked at his big bro as if to ask, *Stop this. Pull the bullets out of me. Tell me I'm good.* Big bro rested Larry's head on his lap, looked into his eyes the way brothers look at each other for an offer, a prayer, for an *I love you*, for one last time.

That shit was fucked up. But it's true. And where we come from, there are a lot of fucked up truths, like no one giving two shits about Brooklyn boys from the hood, and people forgetting about Larry way too fast. He only lived in the East for a month before his life was stripped from him. Larry's death made me think about my own mortality a little more. How it was that I didn't get caught in the crosshairs of the gunfire. I wondered when the bullets would come for me. That was a long time ago, but I still remember it like it was yesterday.

The day Larry was murdered, it was business as usual on the block. I was outside with my little brother, Gabriel, and

---

[30] Mary Spicuzza, "Gunfire Kills a Teenager and Shatters an Oasis," *The New York Times* (2004).

our boy Carlos, sitting on the four-step-stoop of my building, talking our shit: girls, sneakers, and basketball.

"Carlos, you gonna dunk today?" I was a self-centered, seventeen-year-old junior in high school, secretly grieving my parent's recent divorce. But I didn't show it though because, I thought, showing emotions was weak.

All I cared about was basketball, and my loyalty was to the block, Sunnyside Avenue, where all my homies lived. That summer, I caught a dunk off a lob on a non-regulation rim in Highland Park, no more than nine feet. But it was enough for me to grow hair on my chest. I was a couple of years older than Carlos and Gabriel, which meant that I had a de facto duty to coach their basketball game.

"Yeah, Imma dunk today," replied Carlos. "I feel it, son. I got my J's on today, and I've been working on my legs at the gym. It's a wrap! You gonna see! Imma show you something, A!"

"Yeah, aight! We gonna see. You gettin taller, but you still need an inch or two to really get up over the rim," I replied.

"Watch, yo! Imma be at least six-two when I'm twenty. And when I get that tall, Imma be wind-millin' it and all types of shit. Imma be a monster out there!" Carlos followed.

Carlos was a straight A student, a couple of inches shorter than me. He was a freshman at Boys and Girls High School, with big dreams of running point guard for the team. Even though he was Dominican and from the same hood, he was born here. His parents were still together which sometimes made Gabriel and me feel like we lived in two separate worlds.

Carlos might have been younger, but he had a more mature game. He was about playing to win, playing for the team. I only cared about looking nice, breaking ankles and catching bangers.

Gabriel stood idly listening. His game was similar to mine: a lot of dribbling and no jump shot. Perhaps that was the only thing I ever taught him. But he had more heart than me. I played for a moment of glory, a spin move into a shamgod, then a hezy to make you jump. I didn't even care about scoring. If I made you dance, made you believe that I was going left, that I was going up, and you bought it, I won. But Gabriel was a scorer. At five seven, he played like a big man in the post, rocking his skinny frame under the backboard for an easy layup.

"Yo, I was watching this ESPN special last night," Gabriel said, grabbing Carlos' Spalding, "about the top ten dunks of the year, and the commentator said that the trick to the windmill is that you start rotating before your feet get off the ground. Then you'll have time to make that whole windmill. So, if you jump with one foot," he continued turning to me, "you have to rotate the ball at least 180 degrees before you get off the floor."

"That's wack!" Carlos interrupted. "Sounds like some Payless windmill to me. I like a windmill with hangtime, Vice Carter type shit, the whole mill in the air; you feel me?"

Gabriel dismissed Carlos's comment with his hands, hopped off the stoop and ran toward the five-foot fence separating the building from the sidewalk. He held Carlos's ball tight between his hands and rotated his arms 180 degrees and jumped, slamming the ball on the building's gate. He sent an echoing rattle throughout the stretch of the rusted divide that shook the lid off the garbage cans nearby.

"BANG! In yo face! You feel that, son. That's some free advice for your ass right there!" Gabriel shouted.

"You aint shit!" Carlos returned and busted into laughter.

"You look mad stupid doing that right there. You can keep your ESPN advice," I said, as Gabriel extended two middle fingers in our direction.

The thing is Gabriel wasn't completely wrong about the windmill. But he forgot to add an important detail. Starting the windmill on the ground works if you are a one-leg jumper like Lebron James. When Lebron does his signature cock-back dunk, the one where he glides in the air looking like superman and the Statue of Liberty all at once, he does it off the one foot. There's force, strength, agility, and toughness to the one leg dunker. But we can't forget about the two-legged dunker. Take most of MJ's dunks. When he goes up, he transfers momentum into vertical height, using a diagonal stance to take off like a rocket. The two-leg jumper is elegant in the in-flight, displays hang time, and artistry. The two-leg jumper dribbles like AI midair, making everyone watching believe in a higher power. For this jumper, the windmill starts in the torso and then comes down and around more completely.

"You know who's mad tall for his age?" Gabriel said, turning to Carlos. "That new kid, Larry. He like six one, and he only fifteen."

"Too bad he can't dunk though," replied Carlos, "What I wouldn't give to be that tall right now."

"The kid is mad young. He like 15 or somethin. He needs to work on his game. And plus, he moved from some Queens-ass neighborhood just a month ago. He needs to get his inner-beast up. But he got some game. He just needs time," I said.

The truth was that I wished I had Larry's height too. At five ten, I wouldn't grow an inch taller, and my hops didn't give me the power of flight like Lebron James. Oh, and on top of all that, I was a one-leg jumper with weakened ankles. So, everything I did in the air was just forced and angry, and it had an approaching time limit.

"You know, I saw him the other day riding his bike with his big bro. Man, I tell you, his big bro, now that kid look like he a fucking gangsta," Carlos said.

"I wouldn't mess with him. He's what, like twenty or something," I responded. "A grown ass man!"

At home, I didn't have a frame of reference for manhood. Papi left the house earlier that year. Mami found out he had this young girlfriend in DR, who he visited on his *dique* business trips. Papi wasn't even slick about it. He brought her to the house in Hato Mayor, introduced her around town. Who knows, maybe, Gabriel and I have some half-brother out there. Hit me up fam!

Well, Mami wasn't having that shit. She wasn't going to be the immigrant wife who got cheated on, while living in Brooklyn on food stamps and a Section-8 apartment. When Papi left the apartment, he didn't say goodbye. He just packed a bag and dipped. But by then Gabriel and I were committed to the hood, and being sad about our parent's divorce wasn't happening.

With no pop at home, my frame of reference for manhood was in the streets. Twenty-year-olds just seemed old to me, like someone with kids or with a criminal record or someone dead. There weren't twenty-year-old role models in my hood, no one I could look up to say, that's who I want to be. Truth is, I didn't think much about my future. Back then all I cared about were fast breaks to the nine-foot rim, enough run up to leap and catch one, just one good one, preferably in front of girls.

"Larry is young though. You might think he is older than his brother because he's so tall. Especially from far away, he look like a real-ass baller" I replied. "But he aint much younger than you guys," I continued turning to Carlos and Gabriel.

Carlos's and Gabriel's basketball shorts came down below their knees. Carlos rocked a Miskeem shirt with its signature splattered paint design of a hand in thick brush strokes that beckoned you to stop or give it a high five. Gabriel and I loved that shirt. We envied Carlos for not just owning it but for carelessly bouncing a basketball so close to it. For me and Gabriel, a shirt like that was saved for a party or the first day of school. Gabriel and I wore oversized white t-shirts we got from The Spot, 3 for $10.

"I heard he Blood or that his brother Blood or something like that," said Carlos, bouncing the ball between his legs without looking down.

His handles were getting better. There was some elevation in the bounce that sat on his shoulder and then came down rhythmically with his chest. There was confidence in it.

"Yeah, yeah, whateva. Everybody and they momma be Blood or Crip nowadays, Latin King or something. That's how it is in this hood," replied Gabriel as he attempted to strip the ball away from Carlos, who stared down his defender then maneuvered the ball in and out of Gabriel's reach.

"You reach. I teach," Carlos said.

I reclined on the stoop steps watching Gabriel reach and reach while Carlos bounced from left to right, just out of Gabriel's hands.

"I don't think Larry Blood. His brother might be, but I don't know them like that to really say. I know they hang out with Cory, and I think he Blood or at least he rocks a flag and pretends to be," I returned.

Thing is, I didn't really know if Cory was blood either. One day Cory showed up to the park alone. A red bandana hung from his left pocket. Had I met him anywhere else outside of Highland Park, I might've been shook. The memory of Bloods jumping me in Junior High School was tattooed on my brain. But in the park, I was protected. I was the Kid with the Yellow shorts, and no one fucked with the regulars.

Carlos continued dribbling the ball. He tried hitting Gabriel with Iverson's crossover. The most famous version must be against the Bulls in 1997, when AI hit MJ with it. Standing six inches above Iverson, MJ guards AI's left side. AI steps back, bounces the ball from left to right to see if MJ bites. He doesn't and settles into a defensive stance. AI goes for it again. He bounces the ball with his left hand, extends his arm out like he was hugging the air, leans his shoulder, his back and head, his body. The entire world is going left. Then, when the mirage is visible and MJ reaches for the ball, AI answers, swinging the ball back to his right, open, for an easy mid-range.

"Ah! Watch out for that one," Carlos said, a mischievous smile on his face. Gabriel finally slapped the ball from Carlos's control.

"Now, it's your turn to get crossed up," Gabriel said to Carlos as the ball bounced between his legs and around his back. His left-hand needed work, but he was getting it. I watched them, waiting for my turn.

"When I saw Larry yesterday, he and his big bro came up to me, and I didn't know what to expect. I thought shit was going to pop-off. You know people can't just be rolling up on you like they know you. But they were mad chill. Especially Larry. Homie just wanted to know if I played ball and video games. I'm telling you; he just a kid."

Carlos looked at me with probing eyes, "And what? You not a kid like us anymore? You a grown-ass man now?"

I smirked and replied, "Hell yeah, son!"

"Get the fuck out of here!" Carlos followed, as he slapped the Spalding from Gabriel's weak left hand.

"And I got a left hand, watch this," Carlos said while dribbling the ball to his left side and swinging it behind his back to his right side. Looking up from all the movement, he said, "What you know about that?"

"You aint shit!" I said mockingly, smiling and elbowing Gabriel. "He think he Hot Sauce and shit."

"Whateva yo! Whateva! You know I got mad skillz," Carlos returned, dragging the "s" into a "z" sound.

"Aight then, Lets hit up Highland Park, and see who's there," Gabriel returned.

"Sounds good," I said.

We hopped off the four-step stoop and ran toward the end of Sunnyside Avenue. We took turns dribbling the ball, fast breaking down a full court, as if our team was down by one in the fourth quarter, approaching the final seconds on the clock.

"Yo! Pass the rock," I shouted. "Let me see that!"

Carlos passed me the ball. I caught it, running in front of Gabriel. I shot him an under the leg pass I saw Jason Kidd do one time against the Kings. Gabriel received it with his right hand, and with seconds on the clock, we continued all the way to Highland Park.

The sun was barely visible. The July air was finally cooling down, perfect temperature for a night game. The park regulars were shooting for teams. We walked on the courts with the confidence that comes with belonging, the knowledge that we were from there, that everyone there knows what block we're from, who our parents were, and what country we came from. In the park, we didn't have to front like we did in school, wear Jordans that we begged and pleaded our parents to get us, even though they couldn't afford them, just so that we could look like drug dealers, like we mattered.

Youth was an embarrassing thing that wore Jordans. It made you sweat when you walked in a room, hoping, praying, that everyone didn't find out you're faking every step, every swing of your arms, rubbing of the chin, patting of your head, all of it learned from a father, a big bro, some savior athlete walking out from the locker room, rehearsed for that insignificant moment of significance. Nah, the park was our living room with trees and concrete. I know this because at the other end of that embarrassing youth, there is the shame that comes with aging, the feeling of walking onto a court with guys that could be your kids, and hoping, praying that one of them picks you and that they don't call you Unc or OG for the whole game.

"Yo! We playin' too," I said, as daps echoed throughout the court.

"Aight then," Paul said, a local kid from down the street. "We shooting for captains. Shoot after me."

I missed the free throw and blamed it on the wind. Carlos drained his free throw. If the rims had nets, you would've heard a crisp swish. He picked me and Gabriel and two other scrubs who couldn't really play. But it didn't matter. Our Sunnyside crew had enough game to win even with them on the team.

Carlos turned to me, "Aight A, it's game time. We playin man. You guard up Larry's big bro, and I'll guard Paul. Gabriel, you got Red Shorts. Watch for his midrange."

We took our positions. Ball went in, and we ran up and down that court like it was a playoff game.

In the near distance, park pigeons frantically flapped their wings as two BMX bikes rode through. Larry rode his bike behind Cory's toward the basketball courts, their tires nearly shaved to the inner tube from all the racing and tire burning. Perhaps they talked about how hot it was, about who was faster.

"Ya' need an AC in your room. It's too hot to be playin PlayStation," Cory said to Larry. "I don't know how you can spend that much time sitting in front of that hot ass TV all day. You crazy, son."

"It ain't that hot. I like video games, and it only just got hot. I was chilling," returned Larry.

Larry sped in front of Cory. His left foot slipped off the pedal.

"You about to bust your ass," Cory shouted, laughing."
Larry regained his balance, beating Cory to the court entrance.

"Yo! Larry! Let's chill right here while I roll up," Cory
said, pulling out a nickel bag of regs and a Dutch Master from
his basketball shorts.

"Yo, your big bro running a full. Imma call next game,"
Cory continued.

"Aight, do your thing. But I don't feel like playin today,
but go ahead call next," Larry followed.

"Don't give me that shit," said Cory, as he walked toward
the speeding bodies on the court. "Ay, yo! I got next game!"

Larry dropped his bike and sat on the bench facing the
courts. Behind him stood a ten-foot fence of woven steel. Larry
slapped his bike's pedal and watched as its reflectors spun,
picking up that last bit of the day's sun into a perfect halo of
light. Cory sat back down and disemboweled the Dutch
Master, spilling its guts on the ground. He crushed dry buds
and sprinkled them into the cigar's leaf and then unhurriedly
rolled it.

On the court, I looked for any and every opportunity to
dunk the ball on the rim facing the north side of the park, the
significantly lower rim, but couldn't find the right moment. I
baby-sat that side of the court for two plays until Carlos told
me to get back on defense.

"Yo! A! That shit's going to cost us the game. Think of
the team, son," Carlos warned.

We were down four, which, in a street ball game, where
we only go by ones and twos, was like being down by twenty.
But we had heart and weren't about to give up.

Carlos called for the rock and drained a deep one from the top of the key, reducing the lead by two. On the sideline benches, Larry and Cory watched the game and passed a fleeting L around. I knew in the back of my mind that Cory was trying to convince Larry to play.

"Why don't you feel like playing today, my G?" asked Cory. "I mean, why we even here if not to bust some ass?"

"I don't know, man," Larry responded, lightly pulling the Jay. "I just want to chill and watch. To be honest, I only came to shoot around a lil and maybe get a dunk in. I know I can dunk the ball. I got the height and the hops. I just need to do it."

I could feel Larry's eyes watching us run down the court. Paul beamed a baseline pass to Larry's big bro who clutched it with his left hand, his foot an inch from stepping out of bounds. Big bro faked a shot, but I didn't bite. He then sidestepped to his right and pulled a fade-away three. I jumped and extended my arm like Mister Fantastic, blocking nothing but air. The ball banked into the rim.

"Ayy!" Larry shouted as big bro ran back on defense. Larry turned to Cory and said, "How much you wanna bet that Imma catch a banger today?"

"Oh, that's how you feelin now. Ha, ha, ha! Aight" replied Cory. We gonna see, two dollars, I bet you two dollars you ain't dunking that ball today. Deal?"

"Aight, bet," returned Larry.

Between a play, I overheard Cory say, "Yo, there go Blue with that bitch from the other day," pointing his chin beyond the fence.

Anthony approached the left-wing entrance of Highland Park. He was a twenty-three-year-old local Puerto-Rican cat that everyone called Blue because he was Crip. I took the A train with him, sometimes, on my way to school. We talked basketball and sneakers, kept it brief on my express stop to the Utica Avenue Station. But Blue did like to start shit. One time, he told Derek, a Trinidadian kid from around the way, that I was trying to fuck his girl, Steph, a Columbian dime whose parents had on permanent lock down. I did try to get Steph's number one time, but I didn't know she had a man. Steph didn't give me the light of day, and I forgot all about that. Blue showed up with Derek to my block and made us shoot the fair one on the street. I didn't feel like fighting Derek, but my homies were around, and he disrespected the block by simply showing up. So, we fought bareknuckle on the street, until Blue separated us, his eyes full of glee and exhilaration. He really enjoyed seeing us bleed.

Blue rode in the park on a blue freestyle bike with two pegs on the back rim, on which a homegirl of his stood. She held on to Blue's back, just over the strings of his Nike backpack. On the court, we continued running up and down trying to cut our deficit. Gabriel went for a mid-range jump shot but missed. Red Shorts had him locked up with defense.

"Play his right side," Carlos advised Gabriel as he jetted down the court. "He keeps making you go left into the defense."

The blue-bike duo came to a stop behind Larry and Cory, nothing but the porous fence dividing them.

"Yo, bitch!" Blue shouted loud enough for all of us to hear.

"You tried to holla at my boy's girl, cuz," said Blue to Cory, as he pulled off his stringed Nike backpack, and dug through it like he'd lost something deep inside.

"What the fuck is you talking about?" returned Cory, dismissing him with his hands and keeping his eyes on Blue's backpack. Larry said nothing. He barely looked back at Blue who continued mining his bag.

"You ain't gonna say shit, cuz! I know you think you Blood or some shit," Blue followed.

The riff raff on the sidelines made us stop the game. It was obvious that some shit was about to pop off.

"Yo, they about to get it poppin," someone said.

Larry's big bro, confused and tired from running up and down the court, looked toward the commotion.

He collected his breath and shouted to Blue, "Ay yo! What's brackin, Blood!"

The girl that rode with Blue was no more than fifteen years old. She had on gold hoop earrings and a Baby Phat Farm t-shirt that hugged her chest. She hopped off the bike's pegs and shouted, in a general direction, as if berating the park trees in front of her, "What you gonna say now. You don't remember calling me a bitch. You don't know who you fuckin with!"

Blue dug deeper into his Nike bag and pulled out a Baby 9mm.

"What now!?" he yelled.

Cory and Larry were stunned and didn't move from the bench. Blue shot twice into the air, and Cory ran for cover. I don't know why, but Larry stayed, sitting there. Maybe he was frozen with fear. Maybe he didn't want to look like a punk in front of the park. Maybe he thought that Blue wasn't stupid enough to actually shoot at him. I don't know why Larry sat there. But I wish he had moved. I wished he had run for cover like Cory. Jumped out of that bench and joined most of us into adulthood.

"You think this is a game, cuz," continued Blue.

He took aim and shot several times towards Larry's direction. The bullets entered the fence, a couple ricocheting off the jungle gyms and concrete. Some of us ducked and dropped to the ground. Others jumped and ran in a panic. This was the closest we'd ever been to war.

"He shootin with a BB gun, son. Oh shit, Blue's fucking crazy," someone on the court said.

"That ain't a BB gun, my G," someone else corrected.

Larry fell over from the bench and moaned softly over the hard pavement. He tried to get up but couldn't.

I ran from behind the jungle gym toward Larry.

"Yo, Blue, chill, chill son!" I shouted.

Blue picked up his bike, and, out of fear or instinct, who knows, aimed the gun at me, pulled the trigger, but nothing. He emptied the cartridge moments earlier into the air, park, and Larry's teenage body. One bullet lodged in Larry's spine. Another punctured his left lung. Big bro lifted Larry's t-shirt off his back where two small holes dotted his otherwise pristine back. Like eyes streaming red tears, the tiny cavities cried. Big bro turned Larry on his side, and the park stood motionless, wondering if this is what death looked like.

Paul and Red Shorts ran to Larry's house to tell his parents what happened. Time sped up. The park lights came on, and the sun was gone. People came outside, some poked their heads out of their windows to get a good look. Moments later, Larry's mom ran in the park. I didn't see her arrive. We could hear police sirens in the distance as we walked out of the park. From the park's entrance, we heard Larry's mom's cry, her back flashing like a siren.

On the block, we sat on the four-step stoop, not saying a word. The night was cooling down and the sounds of sirens were muffled by other sounds, the traffic of the avenue, people talking in the streets, Luis Vargas blaring from a neighbor's window, and the barely audible wind in the leaves.

When we did open our mouths, we didn't say much, just kept repeating trite clichés: "that was crazy," "damn, son, shit be wild," "man, man, he really shot em." There were no words that could hold that moment together, and what it became, as we grew up and moved in the world, was better left unsaid.

Carlos looked at me and Gabriel, "Yo, I left my ball at the park, son."

It felt like he took our breaths away. "Leave that shit," I replied. "You can have mine."

A stray cat walked by the gate of the building. Its tail was missing. White patches dotted its black fur. It stopped in front of us, and we watched it watch us.

"Damn," Gabriel said, breaking our trance. "Larry was tall enough to dunk. He was getting there, growing a little taller each day, until, boom, bang, slam-dunk, in your face, get up son! He was gonna be nice."

6

The cradle rocks above an abyss, and common sense tells us that our existence is but a brief crack of light between two eternities of darkness. Although the two are identical twins, man, as a rule, views the prenatal abyss with more calm than the one he is heading for (at some forty-five hundred heartbeats an hour).

Vladimir Nabokov[31]

I imagine that by fashioning a title like *Speak, Memory*, the celebrated Russian realist Vladimir Nabokov commanded his memory to give something up, a glimpse of a past life. I ask my *memoria* to do the same, *pero en español*.[32] My task is to translate what most writers wait until they're much older and more accomplished to write. I might not get much older nor more accomplished. So here goes. I write with nothing to lose and without asking too much of my memory. I write as I heal, maybe to heal.

In my mind, Nabokov is right. I've always felt that my cradle is my coffin, that the only thing separating me from eternity is this brief existence. There was darkness in the beginning, but it was calm and apolitical, a steady purity of

---

[31] Vladimir Nabokov, *Speak, Memory* (1987).

[32] Memory, but in Spanish.

nothingness. I think what comes after will be the same. For those of us waiting in the realm of existence, our "prenatal abyss," our not-being-here-yet because you'd never been, was never a tragedy. So why is it that death scares us so much?

I think of my daughter. Before she was born, pulled from the arbitration of darkness, assembled from scattered jigsaws of DNA, the idea of her not-yet-being did not scare me. But now that she is here, that we all are, in this "brief crack of light between two eternities of darkness," the postnatal abyss seems cruel. It's the knowing, the awareness of the abyss—the coming out of its deep pool still soaked with absence—that troubles my mind, my memory that so desperately wants to keep everything.

My earliest years are like anyone else's, both distinct and blurry, as memories tend to be when we try to pin them down. One thing I know for sure: I was a happy, healthy child. We weren't rich in material things, but we had each other, and that was more than enough, even when sometimes having each other felt like the hardest thing.

I was born in 1987 in Jagua, a small farm town near Juncalito, nestled in the municipality of Jánico, in the Dominican Republic. My family had been cultivating that land for over 250 years, growing coffee beans and whatever else the earth would offer. The tradition of being an *agricultor* runs deep in our veins, passed down from generation to generation, yet you could say it died with me when we moved to New York City. Still, the coffee—the smell, the taste, the heritage—remains alive in me.[33]

Ask a Dominican in New York City about Jánico, Juncalito, or Jagua, and you might get a knowing nod, a smile of recognition, or they might look at you like you're the biggest hick to step foot in the U.S.

Jánico is the kind of place where memories linger in the soil, even when you've left. It's more than just a dot on a map; it's a place with a rich colonial history that stretches back centuries. In March 1494, Christopher Columbus himself established a stockade there, driven by the lure of gold hidden within the mountains. This land, brimming with *dique* untold riches, was part of Spain's earliest efforts to colonize the Americas. The first inland fortress on Hispaniola, the Santo Tomás de Jánico Fortress, was built around 1510–1511to protect interior treasures. Though its remains are still visible today, they're fragments of that original structure. The town's name, taken from the old Janicus River—likely a Latinized version of an Arawakan name now lost to history—survives like a whisper of a past that never quite fades.

By the mid-sixteenth century, the Arawakan-speaking Taíno peoples who once inhabited the region known as La Sierra—where Jánico lies—had been largely displaced or decimated by forced labor, disease, and outright violence during the early Spanish conquest. A century later, under the colonial governance of Spanish Governor Antonio de Osorio, the Spanish forcibly depopulated the western and northern parts of the island, including nearby areas, in pursuit of centralized control and to curb contraband trade. As a result,

---

[33] Farmer.

La Sierra never developed a plantation-based economy like the coastal lowlands. Instead, it evolved into a mountainous refuge characterized by small-scale agriculture and relative isolation. By the eighteenth century, the Sierra had become home to an endogamous community of Canarian and French settlers. These immigrants formed a close-knit, insular community, often marrying within their group to preserve their European lineage. During the Haitian Revolution, the Sierra became a sanctuary for waves of white and mulatto refugees fleeing the battles in Saint-Domingue, further reinforcing its character as a culturally distinct enclave in the Dominican interior.

On the drives into Juncalito, it always felt like we were scaling a mountain, and that's because we essentially were. Juncalito is at the highest point of Santiago de los Caballeros, about 100 miles from *La Capital* in the northern part of Hispaniola.[34] The SUV rocked left and right, while I wondered when we would capsize.

How can I describe this place to you? It is a charming little place, heightened by the earth's curve. Think of a landscape painting, an impressionist farm town by Cézanne. Then, I'll start by describing the wind—always calm, a breeze delicate on your sunlit skin, carrying the aroma of mango trees. Smell *el moro de habichuelas y pollo guisado*, or whatever is cooking over the *fogón*, the wild and colorful *Coralillos* growing everywhere, and the sweetness of the orange orchards surrounding the town.[35]

---

[34] The Capital.

[35] Rice and beans with stewed chicken; mud stove.

Hear the Río Bao's waters streaming, clashing against the translucent rocks, the countless birds chirping, *los niños jugando bellugas*, the adults contemplating politics or religion, the hum of a 1970s motorbike, and the sound of church bells.[36] In the middle of this *pintura*, you will see the town church, known for its humble elegance, *La Iglesia de Juncalito*.[37] It stands tall because the ground beneath it stands tall. The sun ignites the color of the old paint, brightening the off-white of the walls. Mango-colored steeples crown the church. It is grand, but not in the European or American sense of the word. It is *grande* in the Dominican sense. This church stands elevated amidst *un campo viejo*.[38] Churchgoers come in their Sunday best to kneel within its walls, praying to Jesus that this year will yield more crops than the last.

Around the steeples, smaller homes stand out, their zinc rooftops gleaming with the amber rust of time. On warm summer nights, the rain taps softly against the metal, a soothing rhythm. The wooden exteriors of these homes are painted in shades of turquoise and sea green, a striking contrast to the muted dirt roads that wind through the town. The faces of Juncalito, filled with friendly curiosity, might glance your way. They might even share a *cuento*, a tale of folk culture passed down through generations—perhaps of *la bruja* dressed all in white, or the story of *el borracho*, who, in a drunken

---

[36] The children playing marbles.

[37] Painting, the Church of Juncalito.

[38] Big, this church, an old countryside.

stupor one day, stumbles upon the ghost of an old friend, too drunk to realize the man has been dead for years.[39]

I remember most of all the people's hospitality, their simple *generosidad*.[40] "*Ten', coje e'ta cosita,*" expecting nothing in return.[41] Many there believed that people were naturally good. These Dominican faces politely measured you up as you measured their town. It's a simple existence with the complexities of a full life.

There are those who might judge you for the color of your skin, for anti-blackness cannot escape even the most remote places. It's the type of racism that comes with a deep colonial past and a racially entangled present, an integrated family of Black cousins, biracial aunts, and white mothers. The racism in these small Dominican towns is not like the one I've experienced in Brooklyn where anti-blackness is plaited with class. Somehow in Brooklyn, even getting a cup of coffee at a café feels like buying into whiteness. Pumpkin spice latte, anyone?

Let's not get it twisted: anti-blackness exists everywhere, and Dominicans have a long and ugly history with it, marked by violence, exile, oppression, and genocide. The same goes for *el sexismo*, a plague that refuses to fade in a country with one of the highest femicide rates in Latin America. I grew up with an elaborate *sistema de castas*, reflecting deep-seated colorism, that categorizes our race into non-Black racial labels

---

[39] A story, the witch, the drunkard.

[40] Generosity.

[41] Take this little thing.

like, *trigueño, canela, indio, moreno, prieto, rubio, blanco*, and so on.[42]

In her study of Spanish America and the concept of *limpieza de sangre* (purity of blood), historian María Elena Martínez traces the *sistema de castas* to the idea of "purity of blood" tied to Catholicism, where the whiter you were, the closer you were to both Spanishness and God.[43] Others, including Ginetta E. B. Candelario and Anne Eller, link anti-blackness to the anti-Haitianism that emerged before, during, and after the 22 years of Haitian unification of Hispaniola, when President Jean-Pierre Boyer abolished slavery, redistributed the lands of the Catholic church and caudillos to the poor and formerly enslaved, and imposed heavy taxes on the Spanish side that, largely, suppressed Dominican autonomy and cultural identity.[44] But, as Silvio Torres-Saillant points out, anti-Haitianism wasn't simply a nineteenth-century phenomenon.[45] The institutionalization of anti-Haitianism during Rafael Leonidas Trujillo's dictatorship sought to cement Haitians as the official antithesis of the Dominican state.

---

[42] Caste system, dark-skinned, cinnamon-colored, Indian, dark-skinned, dark-skinned, blond, white.

[43] María Elena Martínez, *Genealogical Fictions: Limpieza de Sangre, Religion, and Gender in Colonial Mexico* (2008).

[44] Ginetta E. B. Candelario, *Black Behind the Ears: Dominican Racial Identity from Museums to Beauty Shops* (2007); Anne Eller, *We Dream Together: Dominican Independence, Haiti, and the Fight for Caribbean Freedom* (2016).

[45] Silvio Torres-Saillant. "Homeland, Poetry, and Justice: Julia Álvarez Engages Pedro Mir." *Afro-Hispanic Review* (2013).

One of the most infamous expressions of anti-Haitian sentiment was the 1937 Parsley Massacre, a brutal act of ethnic cleansing along the Haiti–Dominican Republic border. Trujillo's soldiers held up sprigs of parsley and asked Black people to name it. If the person responded by trilling the 'r' in perejil, ninthey were free to go. Those who couldn't, mostly Haitian Kreyòl speakers, were assumed to be Haitian and were likely killed.

But the idea that Trujillo's soldiers stopped each Black person they encountered, mostly sugarcane farmers from border towns, to test their pronunciation is unlikely. Many were slaughtered on sight, hacked with machetes where they stood. Others were pushed off cliffs and landed on jagged rocks; those who survived the fall were met with machetes on the shore.

In *The Farming of Bones*, Edwidge Danticat renders the brutality and inhumanity of the killings. She shows how Haitian workers heard whispers of what was coming, how some tried to flee across the border, others sought refuge in churches. The Haitian government, particularly President Sténio Vincent, did little. They accepted Trujillo's $750,000 in reparations—blood money—most of which never reached the victims' families.

Danticat's protagonist, Amabelle, reflects:

> Que diga amor? Love? Hate? Speak to me of things the world has yet to truly understand, of the silent meaning of each bird's calls, of a child's secret thoughts in her mother's womb, of the measured, rhythmical time of every man and woman's breath, of the true colors of the inside of the moon, of the larger miracles in small things, the deeper mysteries. But

parsley? Was it because it was so used, so commonplace, so abundantly at hand that everyone who desired a sprig could find one? We used parsley for our food, our teas, our baths, to cleanse our insides as well as our outsides. Perhaps the Generalissimo, in some larger order, was trying to do the same for his country.[46]

And indeed, he did intend to use Haitians—a practice that continues to this day. According to a U.S. Department of Labor–sponsored report, "Individuals of Haitian origin or descent make up the majority of the sugarcane workforce in the Dominican Republic."[47] In this way, the name "Haiti" became—and remains—synonymous with cheap labor and a deep-rooted historical hatred that has yet to be fully confronted.

Of course, we shouldn't think of anti-Haitianism as an isolated event in Hispaniola. It's part of a larger narrative of racism that is intertwined with global anti-blackness and white supremacy, fueled by capitalism and Westernization. I believe the Dominican understanding of race and blackness is shaped by all of the above, as well as the personal experiences of Dominicans both on the island and within the diaspora.

Although my family regularly and explicitly talked about race—who was lighter and who was darker, who looked white or who looked Haitian—we never talked about racism. All I knew was that my grandmother was Black. Mami was

---

[46] Edwidge Danticat, *The Farming of Bones* (1998).

[47] U.S. Department of Labor, Bureau of International Labor Affairs. "Supply Chain and Forced Labor Study in the Sugarcane Industry of the Dominican Republic." U.S. Department of Labor (2023).

white (or white-looking, at least). That was clear. But we were blood, and that was all that mattered.

It wasn't until later in life that words like *morenito* and *indio* began to carry weight, when I saw Dominicans kick dirt at Haitian vendors, yelling *Monsieur* and *Madame* with Dominican accents. It wasn't until I moved out of New York and to Ohio that these once-blurry concepts began to solidify, and the sharp divisions they brought started to slice through my understanding of the world.

This was long before I left the cocoon of Juncalito— the Río Báo, its tributary creeks, where rocks nestled crabs beneath jeweled streams. I was born near that mango-steepled, river-scented town. The little *casita* where I lived for the first two years of my life sat on the outskirts, in Jagua Arriba, on the sierra where farmers like Papi and his father grew coffee beans, yuca, plantains, and *verduras*.[48] Beyond Juncalito, dirt roads lead to greener, smaller places like Jagua Abajo and Cuchilla—places you get to by footpaths that grow thinner, steeper, more intimate.

The perfume of Caribbean pines instinctively signifies safety—a kind of safety you can't capture in a photograph or even in writing. I could carefully describe to you what it felt like to walk those pine-needled paths, the taste of every fruit growing in those orchards. But you wouldn't feel what I feel for that place. This place marks the beginning of my family's *cuento*.

Think of a small cabin in the woods, maybe in Upper Michigan, but don't conjure up Hemingway's father's place, because it was nothing like that. Ours was more like a shack,

---

[48] Vegetables.

an assortment of wood, recycled and gathered, to lift four walls, two rooms, and zinc roof with campesino hands and prayers that the structure would hold through humidity and hurricane. About an hour's walk from Juncalito, our *casita* in Jagua Arriba was a simple rural dwelling. The land did not cost anything. It belonged to my family. Most of the homes there were dispersed at least a quarter mile from one another, because with the *casitas* came the farming grounds, which varied in size from small Brooklyn parks to vacant parking lots.

Mami and Papi were both born and raised in Jagua Arriba, but their upbringings couldn't have been more different. Mami was dirt poor—literally. The floors of her childhood shack were nothing but packed earth. She came from a big family, six children in all: four sisters and two brothers. Her parents, Mamá Carmita and Papá Agustín, had lost two infants, a tragedy Mami said was all too common in those days. Despite the hardship and sorrow, people found ways to carry on. According to Mami, much of their poverty stemmed from her father's lack of ambition when it came to providing for the family.

"*Es que a Papi no le gustaba trabajar mucho.*[49] So, it was up to us, the women, to find what we could," Mami would often say.

I wish I knew more about Papá Agustin. I'm sure Mami does too. There is one photo of him that, to me, sums up his character. He is staring intensely at the camera, as if looking through the lens. He has the eyes of a tired man who has suffered yet has loved and has been loved. In the background,

---

[49] Daddy didn't like to work very much.

a dirt path stretches to the sierra, where I imagine the coffee beans blush before picking.

In the early '80s, when Mami was a teenager, schooling didn't mean much unless it was in agriculture. Her family was made up mostly of strong women, and they all had to work. At fifteen, Mami earned sixteen dollars a month working as a live-in maid for a family in Santiago. Her father made monthly trips into the city to pick up her pay and bring her the things she missed from home: clothes, letters, and her family's love.

Papá Agustín hitched rides into Santiago, riding in the bed of his nephew Diogene's Toyota Tacoma. The roads out of Jagua Arriba are treacherous, winding like the rabid waves of a tempestuous ocean. One clear morning, the jolting and shifting of the truck threw Papá Agustín overboard. He died from a severe head injury.

That same afternoon, Diogene arrived in Santiago with Papá Agustín's pine coffin in the back of the truck. When Mami asked who the *difunto* was in the back, he told her it was a relative, without saying more.[50] They drove to Jagua in silence. It was only when Mami arrived home—when she saw the mourners dressed in black, rosaries in hand, and her sisters running toward her with wan, tear-streaked faces, shouting, "Oh, our father, our Papi!"—that she learned her father had died.

Mami has told me this story many times. What she remembers most is running—running toward the sierra, pushing herself under a barbed wire fence, likely cutting her

---

[50] Deceased.

flesh, and tumbling down the hill. She told me she did it because she wanted to die.

"I wanted to be with him," she said.

After Papá Agustin's death, Mami and her three sisters—Brígida, Carmela, and Antonia—along with my two uncles, Anje and Mecho, did their best to keep the household afloat. The loss of their father hit them hard, especially Uncle Mecho. Devastated, he decided to try his luck by traveling illegally to Puerto Rico, crammed into a rickety raft with other hopefuls, guided by smugglers.

He almost made it. Just thirty minutes from the Puerto Rican coast, the authorities moved in to arrest them. But Uncle Mecho was a skilled swimmer. He managed to reach the shore before they could catch him—only to be apprehended and deported back to Hispaniola, returning home with nothing but a story to tell. Luck was clearly not on Mami's family's side. Every attempt at survival was undone by a fate that seemed determined to break them. As Mamá Carmita put it, "marriage was their only salvation."

From Mami's point of view, Papi had everything anyone could dream of. He owned a striking white horse—*La Bestia Blanca*—which he rode proudly through town. Mami used to joke that she fell in love with the horse, not with him.[51]

Papi's father, known to everyone as Chepe, was one of the lucky few from Jagua who had papers and built a life in New York City. Chepe and Mamá Flora, Papi's mother, never married. Their relationship was always described to me as a one-sided fling:

---

[51] The White Beast.

The poor Dominican Black girl, madly in love with a poor farmer, accepts whatever scraps of love he offers.

The poor farmer is a *mujeriego*—part of Dominican manhood, then and now.

The poor girl loses three children in infancy.

One survives (my father).

The poor farmer, with no legal ties to her, emigrates to New York City and starts a new family.

The surviving child (Papi) remains behind—the golden child of the *campo*, forever yearning for his father's affection.

Months before my father was born in 1965, Papá Chepe emigrated to New York City, leaving Papi and Mamá Flora behind. This was a time when there were still very few Dominicans in the city. Through the connections of friends from back home, Papá Chepe found work—hard labor, mostly—and saved what he could to send money back to his son. He promised Mamá Flora that he would arrange for their boy to join him soon, so he could escape the *campo*, too.

But after settling in the U.S., Papá Chepe married and started a new family. He traveled back to the Dominican Republic often, sometimes bringing Papi's half-brothers along for the visits. He would go on to do very well in his new surroundings. He opened a Dominican restaurant just blocks away from Madison Square Garden. He employed his sisters, cousins, and countless Dominican immigrants just starting out in the country.

In my family's lore, Papá Chepe was a hero—a man who lifted so many people out of poverty, including my father. And as much as I loved him growing up—as much as I loved when he hugged me with his big arms and protruding belly, as much as I loved running through his enormous house across from the Brooklyn Public Library on Arlington Avenue—I also felt betrayed by his absence in my father's life. It felt personal, like something he had done not just to my father, but to me. Like something he did again to my own daughter.

In 1989, Papi finally immigrated to the States. He worked for Papá Chepe in his restaurant, mostly as a delivery boy—riding through Midtown Manhattan with styrofoam containers of yuca, fried salami and eggs, *pollo guisado*, *moro de guandules*, and ice-cold *morir soñando* in hand, all while dreaming the dream of bringing his family over one day.[52]

It took Papi only a year to save enough money to move us out of the *campo*. And you wonder why poor people risk their lives to move to the United States. Papi had a house and a *colmado* built in Hato Mayor, in the heart of Santiago, where he moved all of us: me, my brother, Mami, Mamá Flora, and her husband Victor, a local farmer from Jagua, who became the grandfather of my childhood.[53]

Mamá Flora was the strongest person I've ever known. She was always up before the sun and in bed early, never wasting a moment. The memories of her running the *colmado*, managing the shopping for inventory, and still finding time to cook the best Dominican food you've ever tasted, will forever live rent-free in my soul. She was a Afro-Dominicana who never liked to talk about her blackness. There were whispers in the family—rumors that her father, Papá Juan, was Haitian,

---

[52] Stewed chicken, brown rice and beans, "to die dreaming" (milkshake).
[53] Grocery.

and that his sister spoke Spanish with a distinct Kreyòl accent. But as soon as those stories surfaced, they were quickly buried.

I often wondered why we couldn't talk about these things. But it became clear to me as I grew old enough to look—to really look—at the disrespect and outright contempt some Dominicans directed at Haitians. It was in trying to understand that I began to see the jokes about Black skin, the mimicry of Kreyòl accents, the bullying of men and children, the harassment of women—all of it—as part of a fabric of hate, a mantle that stretches across my country. I quickly learned, as my family had known for generations, that being associated with Haitian identity could be dangerous in the Dominican Republic.

Mamá Flora was born in 1940, at the height of Trujillo's reign, just three years after the Parsley Massacre. From the moment Trujillo seized power in 1930 until his assassination in 1961, he waged a campaign of ethnic cleansing. His methods were anything but subtle: massacres, rape, and corruption defined his regime. He was obsessed with "whitening" the Dominican population, openly inviting Europeans to settle while systematically persecuting and killing those of African descent.

The irony was bitter. Trujillo himself had African roots, yet he terrorized the island for over three decades, half of which my grandmother lived through. The *campo* was not spared from his hate-fueled policies. Even there, in the heart of rural life, the shadow of his brutality stretched, leaving no corner untouched.

Mamá Flora would always say that back then, a better life meant simply having enough to eat, a roof over your head, and maybe a little money tucked away for hard times. She told me her upbringing was more secure than most. Her mother, Mamá Lolita—born Angelica Dolores Espinal—was a strict disciplinarian and a devout Catholic. I was fortunate to know her. I remember her caramel skin dotted with liver spots, her long wavy hair—already gray by the time I met her—coiled into a bun each morning and falling loose down her back by evening. Her family was from Cagüeyes, a rural section of the Jánico municipality in Santiago Province. They moved to Jagua Arriba in the 1930s. Mamá Lolita seldom smiled, and when she did, she hid her mouth and teeth with both hands, her eyes glistening. Yet to me, she never felt like some distant great-grandmother from another era, even though she was born in 1920.

Mamá Flora liked to remind us that when she was young, every night in their four-room shack, her mother made the young children pray the rosary. Mamá Flora had nine siblings and they all had to recite *Padre Nuestro*.[54] None of the children received much schooling. Mamá Flora only completed second grade before she was needed in the house to fetch water from the river, sweep the floors, and shell beans. The men were farmers, like most men in Jagua Arriba.

Mamá Flora passed away in June 2024, five years after my father—her only son—died of glioblastoma. But Papi wasn't the only child she lost. There were three others, all babies, who died before their first birthdays, including a little girl named Altagracia.

Mamá Flora's death came as no surprise. After Papi died, every time I spoke to her, all she could talk about was dying,

---

[54] Our Father.

how there was nothing left for her in this world. Although she wasn't particularly religious, I believe she saw death as her best chance at seeing her son again.

Papi and Mamá Flora's relationship was perhaps the strongest example of mother-son love I've ever witnessed. They spoke every day, at work, at home. He flew to the Dominican Republic at least once a year just to see her. And when Papi finally became a U.S. citizen, he arranged her travel papers so she could visit him. Less than a year later, he died. At his funeral, Mamá Flora kept repeating through sobs, "You brought us here, only to leave us."

Papá Victor had ten siblings, not counting two, he said, who died before he was born. "Back then," he once told me, "people had a lot of kids because we didn't have television. Folks had to keep themselves entertained somehow." When I asked him about school, he said, "I went, but I didn't learn anything. Children went maybe once or twice a week because we were needed at home for chores and work. By the time I returned, I was already behind, completely disconnected from what the teacher was teaching. So I left school, probably around the same time Flora did."

"And your parents?" I asked. "Did they care about your education?" "No," he replied. "It was a different time. Parents didn't care much about school."

When I ask about his upbringing, his words are sparse, as if he's digging for something long buried. "Things were different back then," he says. "There was a lot of poverty. We didn't know anything."

I once asked if he was happier then. He paused on the phone before saying, "In some ways, I felt good and safe. There was no crime. But there were many difficult moments. We had nothing, barely enough to eat." And when I bring up politics, he redirects the question to me: "Could you imagine how it was with that man in power?"

I try to fill in the gaps; the fear they must have lived with, especially Mamá Lolita and her family, but really, all Black Dominicans. When I say this aloud, Papá Victor nods. "Well, you already know that's the truth."

For many Dominicans of the Trujillo generation, the trauma of that regime—the policing of thought, the disappearances, the fear of imprisonment and death—still lingers. Somehow, it's been passed down, especially in the literature we write. Trujillo's tyranny, his lust, his anti-Haitianism, they appear again and again. I've always said that Trujillo is a form of inherited trauma Dominincas haven't figured out how to shake, whether on the island or in the diaspora.

The years leading up to Mamá's death were hard on Papá Victor's aging body. He was her sole caretaker, cooking for her, feeding her, bathing her. And when she could no longer walk, he lifted her into bed each night. She was the love of his life, he told me. He did everything he could for her. I can't imagine what it felt like to know she was ready to leave, even if it meant leaving him alone.

Mami once told me how much she loved going to school as a little girl, but her parents couldn't afford books for all six children, who were close in age. They had to share what little they had. Mamá Carmita would carefully divide the pages of a single notebook, so each child had an equal share.

Mami's school was a forty-minute walk from home, along dirt hills and paths, past barbed wire fences, and even across a river. I know, I know. What Caribbean kid hasn't heard this formulaic story before? For Mami, school was like a game of pretend, much like how children play "house" or "hide and seek." It felt like a fantasy world, far removed from the realities of her daily life.

She made it to the fifth grade but couldn't continue because she was needed at home. Daily chores, like walking a mile to fetch water, took priority. Mamá Carmita wanted her children to be educated, but back then, survival meant everyone had to sacrifice something.

Mamá Carmita was one of those Cibaeñas who could, at least through family lore and hearsay, trace part of her lineage back to a Spaniard. According to family stories, her grandmother was a woman named Julia Álvarez—yes, like the celebrated Dominican author but there's no relation. As the tale goes, Julia arrived in the Dominican Republic during the U.S. occupation (1916-1924) and married a local Dominican farmer, adding yet another layer of hardship and resilience to the family's legacy. In my family research, I have not found any evidence of this person ever existing. But as I've learned, archives are often incomplete and insincere, and there's always some truth in oral traditions.

If this all adds up, Julia would've arrived around the time a young Trujillo was rising through the ranks of the U.S. Marines, gradually gaining power and influence on the island. The shadow of his ambition loomed over the country, though no one knew then how dark that shadow would eventually become.

My family's story doesn't explain exactly what brought Julia to the Cibao, or if she truly existed beyond the stories passed down through generations. What is clear is that if she did come, she arrived with nothing and died young, leaving only fragments of her story behind, *pedacitos* woven into the fabric of our family's history.[55]

---

[55] Pieces.

7

Ojalá el otoño en vez de hoja' secas
Vista mi cosecha 'e petit salé
Sembra' una llanura de batata y fresas
Ojalá que llueva café.

Pa' que en el conuco no se sufra tanto, ay ombe
Ojalá que llueva café en el campo
Pa' que en [Jagua Arriba] oigan este canto.[56]

Juan Luis Guerra[57]

Mami always tells me the story of my birth—partly because
it's one she could never forget. She was 19 years old when she

---

[56] The original lyric is "Pa que en Villa Vásquez oigan este canto." I
replace Villa Vásquez with my birth town, Jagua Arriba.

[57] Juan Luis Guerra, "Ojalá que llueva café ," Ojalá que llueva
café (1989).
I hope for autumn instead of dry leaves / look at my harvest of pitisalé
/ sow a plain with sweet potatoes and strawberries / I hope it rains
coffee in the campo. // So that in the *conuco* we won't suffer so much /
I hope it rains coffee in the campo. / So that in [Jagua Arriba] they
hear this / song.

gave birth to me. She was petite, she said, malnourished, and standing at five-foot-nothing. She wasn't ready to give birth to a ten-pound human.

No, I wasn't born in the woods, though that might've made for a better story. I was delivered in a small hospital in Jagua, with the help of real doctors, not medicine men. My umbilical cord, or hers, was certainly cut with surgical scissors and not bitten off, though I'm sure that could've been done. The story goes that the doctor who helped Mami was a heavyset man in his forties. My aunt Brijida was with her, but Papi was out in the fields, working. The nurse who attended to my mother looked at me, then at the doctor, and asked Mami if the doctor was Papi.

Mami and Papi were very poor and didn't own a camera, so there are only a handful of grainy baby photos of me. You'd think I was born in the nineteenth century, when cameras were a luxury.

A strange feeling comes over me when I flip through my partner's baby albums—family albums labeled by year and place—seeing her, who was born before I was, growing up in color photographs. Maybe it's jealousy. Maybe it's heartbreak. Maybe I'm angry at my parents, or at their poverty. Most of all, I think I feel regret. Regret for not having something of my past, some visual evidence, to pass down to my daughter. But my experience isn't unique. That's just how it was. Jagua in the 1980s was basically the nineteenth century. That's how it was in small Dominican towns where electricity and running water were considered luxuries.

My first steps were on dirt floors, which were common in Jagua. Our dirt floors were painted white. It's hard to imagine, but it's true. The house Mami and Papi moved into after I was born had two sections and a *letrina* for a bathroom.[58] The smaller section of the house was the kitchen. The wooden planks that made up the structure had gaps, an inch or two apart, letting sunlight stream through. There was a small window at the end of the kitchen that opened like a treasure chest. The *fogón* always smelled of firewood, and when Mami cooked, smoke and cinders danced in the sunlight seeping through the planks. At night, when the moon was out, the wind whistled through the cracks, and the crickets filled the air with their song.

King of Dirt Floors

I was born king
of dirt floors—
fogón-bright was my life.

In four walls
spread like bad teeth,
I chewed days
that tasted *avena*-white.

We were all
a species of innocent then,
patriotic to those floors
because they were sovereign.

---

[58] Latrine.

Dirt was only so good
to us Dominicans loyal to it.
We swallowed our innocence
with those memories.

We gave up
our dominion
for anything.

Before my brother, Gabriel was born, I remember Mami making *avena* in an old fire-stained pot.[59] I remember the milky vapor and the sound of *el cucharón* making its slow rounds in the foamy ocean of sweetness.[60] Mami fed me while Papi worked the coffee fields. I have this one picture of Mami and me. I must have been one; she looked at me *con una curiosidad* as if shocked that I was hers, that I was an extension of her and the man she loved.[61] I wore a gold crucifix around my neck and stared blankly into the camera.

Papi sometimes took me with him to the coffee fields, a deep mass of dark green shrubbery under a cool canopy. He told me I loved riding with him on his horse. One day, while Papi was working the farm, Mami had to run an errand for Mamá Flora. She left me alone in my cuna, fast asleep.[62]

---

[59] Oatmeal.

[60] Ladle.

[61] A curiosity.

[62] Cuna.

According to Mami, somehow, I managed to climb out of it, crawl out the front door, and make my way into the wide open plain. I crawled ten meters from the house, under a barbed wire fence, and down to a grassy field. Mami, worried sick, claimed to have found me not too far from the coffee fields, among a herd of cows.

One of my earliest memories is of chasing chicks up and down my neighbor's yard, hoping to keep one as a pet. I must have been four. I knew exactly which one I wanted. I remember running, and running, always missing the tiny yellow plumes, and then Mami shouting my name. Before I could stop, I felt something under my right shoe. To my horror, the chick I had chosen was struggling under my foot, gasping for life. Its tiny, disfigured body convulsed until it stopped. I was stunned. It was my first confrontation with death. My parents didn't make much of it. As farmers, they were mostly embarrassed, I'm sure, that I had killed one of their friend's chicks.

It was around this time when Papi started hearing word about his traveling papers. By then Papá Chepe had opened his Dominican restaurant near Madison Square Garden. His restaurant became a popular spot for Dominicans and Latinos in general working in the area. The news of Papi's visa brought excitement to our family. Papi was finally going to America! That meant we were next. It was our way out. Papi's journey to the United States wouldn't be as dramatic as my uncle's to Puerto Rico, but it was no less significant.

One morning, Papi got a call from Papá Chepe with promising updates on his travel arrangements. Chepe explained the immigration process. Papi would need to get his photo taken and prepare for an interview at the American consulate in Santiago. Mamá Flora and Mami were a mix of excitement and anxiety. Sure, they were thrilled, but they also worried. Papi was heading to a completely new world: new people, new culture, a new language. I was too young to grasp what was happening.

A few weeks later, Papi had his interview in Santiago. This interview would decide if he could travel or not. They said it was just a formality, that the American government needed to verify his relationship with Papá Chepe. The truth is, with these interviews, you never really know how things will go. They say it's just routine, a few questions to confirm details, but the immigration process is never that simple. Your visa could hinge on knowing something as random as your father's birthday, the street he grew up on, or the name of the restaurant where he works. The last thing you want is to appear suspicious.

In the vastness of the United States, it's easy to forget the limits of island life. People often visit the Caribbean islands for vacations, admiring the beauty and dreaming of paradise. But few consider the restrictions islanders face, how many are trapped by circumstances, unable to ever leave. For those of us in the Dominican Republic, getting out was a dream, and Papi's papers were our ticket to that dream.

On the day of Papi's interview, the entire town of Jagua Arriba buzzed with a mix of excitement and nerves. Everyone within walking distance of our *casita* came by, eager to hear the news.

Papi, unsure if his memory would hold up during the interview, told Mami and Mamá Flora that if they saw him walking down the dirt road with a suitcase, it meant he had been *visado*.[63] In Jagua, you could spot a traveler from miles away, making their slow journey in or out of town. Papi left early that morning and didn't return until sunset. In the distance, Mamá Flora spotted him—a familiar shadow elongated along the dirt path carefully carrying an oversized suitcase, making sure it didn't touch the dusty road.

His silhouette wasn't just a man returning from an interview; it was a symbol of hope. He represented a fresh start, a new root planted in distant soil, and the promise of what often takes generations to achieve.

Papi has always been a meticulous man, particular about his appearance and belongings, perfectly groomed hair and nails, and that suitcase was no exception. As soon as Mamá Flora saw him with it, tears filled her eyes. She knew at that moment that her son's life was about to change forever, and that soon, we would no longer call this land our home. She rushed inside to tell Mami, who had been waiting for this moment. With joyful tears, she cried, "*¡Visaron a Julito!*" (Papi's nickname).[64] The two most important women in his life ran to greet him, embracing him as the weight of possibility settled in. Soon, the entire town followed, a glint of hope and longing in their eyes.

That night, I imagine, a *merengue tipico* band assembled in the dirt road facing our *casita*. The according and tambora jolted the feets of campesinos who—with every spin—lifted dusty tornados off the dirt road. The headlights of 1970s Volkswagen illuminated portions of the dancing bodies,

---

[63] Obtained a visa.

[64] They approved Julito's visa!

casting long cinematic shadows onto the darkness of the planes. *Romo* spilled from plastic cups, parts evaporating upon impact.[65] Chamaquitos crisscrossed the shadows with alacrity, chasing a never-ending childhood.[66]

Two weeks later, Papi would be on his way to a new life in a country many could only dream of visiting. Perhaps it was nothing but a dream, but I remember him leaving. It was still dark out, and the crickets had kept me up all night. We all slept in the same bed. In my half-asleep state, I thought I heard voices in a dream, but it was Papi getting ready to go, and Mami silently crying beside him.

I woke to the soft glow of a light. Gabrielito was fast asleep. Papi had on his best clothes. Mami was in her *bata*.[67] They were dressed for different journeys, the kerosene lamp illuminating their tear-streaked faces. Naturally, I started crying too. Papi was almost ready. The sun hadn't risen yet, and the roosters were still quiet. His suitcase looked bigger and heavier than the last time I saw it. Both Mami and Papi looked at me as if I were part of this moment and, as confused as I was concerned, I jumped out of bed and ran to him. He knelt down and told me I would see him soon.

In times when I feel my body growing old, my mind growing tired, when I feel very far away from my family, like life's

---

[65] Rum.

[66] Little kids.

[67] Nightgown.

huérfano, I pull at this memory.[68] There's something so soft and fresh in all the promise it held.

When Papi died in April of 2019 from a cruel brain tumor, I turned to this memory of him. His bag packed; his eyes crimsoned with tears. Even though the cancer took his memories, I have a feeling that he knew he was going to a different place, a place he couldn't take us to. The day he died, I wanted to go with him, to keep him company, so that he wouldn't miss the warmth of son's love.

---

[68] Orphan.

8

I am your culebra.
I am in the dirt for you.

Natalie Diaz[69]

In the United States, Papi worked hard as a delivery boy for Papá Chepe's restaurant. He did not make much, but he earned enough to send us something every week.

In those days, Mamá Flora was like my second mother. She always made me smile and reminded me of Papi. I can't picture her without a *cigarillo* between her lips.[70] Gabriel and I mimicked her by rolling paper cigarettes full of dry leaves.

Papá Victor was the grandfather figure of my childhood, and there was something magical about him. Maybe it was his easy going confidence, his sense of humor, or his kind, dark brown eyes. He worked in the quarry in Santiago, and I can still remember him coming home, covered in thick layers of

---

[69] Natalie Diaz, "Post Colonial Love Poem," *Post Colonial Love Poem* (2020).

[70] Cigarettes.

the earth's best *tierra*.[71] The smell of the earth, mixed with a hint of tobacco smoke, became his signature scent.

Once, when I was five, Papá Victor took me to work with him at the quarry. I discovered that deep beneath the surface, the earth turns a rich sepia color. I wanted to dig my hands into the soil, to feel the dampness he unearthed with his shovel and pickaxe.

I remember Papá Victor mixing cement, thinking it was the most interesting thing I'd ever seen. In a mound of soil that looked like a giant anthill, he'd clear a space at the center for the powdered cement. With his rusty shovel, he created music as he shuffled the cement and soil together, lifting and blending the elements with a rhythmic grace, dust swirling around him.

Then came the water, flooding the mixture. Air bubbles, like frantic fire ants, trying to escape, as the sun played tricks on my eyes. Papá Victor kept shuffling with his shovel until the cement thickened into a dough-like consistency. It was a spectacle to watch. You could practically butter a building with that mixture, and once it dried, it would stand tall and firm, strong enough to last for generations.

On Sundays, we visited Mamá Flora's parents, my great-grandparents, Mamá Lolita and Papá Juan. They lived in another part of Santiago, and we'd take a *concho* to get there. [72] For those who don't know, *conchos* are Dominican Ubers before Uber was a thing. The drivers packed in as many passengers as possible, sometimes you'd end up sitting on a

---

[71] Soil.

[72] Dominican public taxi.

stranger's lap, or they on yours, but no one seemed to mind. The rides were always bumpy, with heavy traffic and unbearable heat. The thick scent of gasoline and hot tar filled the air, reminding you that all the windows were down in the struggling car. Pesos jingled in the cigarette tray under the static-filled hum of the radio, while the adults sweated and chatted. Gabriel and I hated those rides and couldn't wait to get to our great-grandparents' house, where we'd run straight to *el colmado* for Coca-Colas.[73]

Mamá Flora's father, Papá Juan, was Haitian and lived to nearly one hundred years old. He seemed like the oldest man in the world. I remember sitting on his lap as he ran his dark brown fingers over my face, murmuring, *"qué niño de Dios."* [74] Mamá Lolita, his wife, passed away just three years shy of her hundredth birthday. She looked much younger than her age and always had sweets ready for Gabrielito and me. They lived on a busy street in La Yagüita de Pastor, in a long, narrow house with a zinc roof. Stray dogs with flies orbiting their genitals roamed outside freely. Their emaciated frames and ribbed tight skin made it hard for them to walk in the heat of summer.

Once a month, Mamá Flora took me to *el mercado.*[75] We arrived early to buy the freshest fruits, vegetables, and meats. *El mercado* was like a festival of colors and smells. People walking to and fro, some yelling out prices, others laughing,

---

[73] Grocery store.

[74] What a child of God.

[75] Market.

some talking amongst themselves. In the emptier areas, one could see cows hauling merchandise too heavy for people to carry. There were also chickens in cages for sale and wild ones in the streets, likely escaping from a careless owner.

Kids grow up faster in the Dominican Republic. At six years old in DR, I craved more freedom than I ever did at nine in Brooklyn. I think it has something to do with a sense of belonging. In the Dominican Republic, I never questioned whether I belonged; it was never a mountain I had to climb.

In Hato Mayor, my best friend was Rony. His family made fireworks, and his older brother, Richard, was a trickster who would throw firecrackers at us while we played. Rony and I were inseparable, going everywhere together. One day, he took me to the tobacco factory a few blocks from my house, right by a riverbank that hadn't quite dried up yet. We spent the afternoon fishing for crabs among the old truck tires and scattered trash.

One afternoon, Rony came by my house carrying supplies for his father. He had stopped by the river, hoping to catch crabs, but instead found a small crawfish. He came up to my gate and said, "*Oye, ten', pa' ti, cúidalo.*" [76] It was the first crawfish I'd ever seen, and I thought it was the most fascinating creature in the world. Rony told me to keep it in a bucket of water if I wanted it to survive. I did as he said, but soon grew bored of watching it do nothing. So, I took it out and let it roam free. That, too, quickly lost its appeal.

And that's when I did the first truly evil thing I can remember. I found a fire ant colony in my front yard, easy to

---

[76] Here, here, this is for you, take care of it.

spot, as those little red devils were everywhere, biting me regularly. I wanted to see the crawfish fight for its life. I placed it on top of what must have looked like a fiery battlefield to its bulging eyes. The ants sensed the threat as my shadow loomed over their sandy fortress. They swarmed, and the crawfish was defenseless.

One little red devil bit me, but I was used to their bites, and I did not want to miss this spectacle. The crawfish twitched and struggled, its claws flailing as the red devils covered it, biting relentlessly. An army of diablos covered the clawed monster and bit it countlessly.[77] It must have boiled with pain on top of the anthill. Watching it squirm, fighting in vain, as its body coiled into a lifeless shape, filled me with guilt. I ran to Papá Victor, crying, horrified by what I had done.

Gabriel would join in my shenanigans and think of semi-evil things to alleviate our boredom, as that was the last crawfish we ever had. We did, however, have many other pets: at least three dogs and a cat that would only show its face when it was hungry or thirsty. Mamá Flora and Papá Victor kept the dogs for protection and the cat for vermin maintenance. We loved the dogs more though. One windy afternoon, Gabriel and I spotted the cat that Papá Victor called *misu* (a term that many Dominicans use to call cats). It rested on the floor of the *galería*, probably enjoying the summer breeze under the shade.[78] Without warning, Gabriel looked at me and said

---

[77] Devils.

[78] Gallery.

"Mira!"[79] He then grabbed the sleepy cat by its tail, swung it once or twice like a feline helicopter starting its engine, and released it into the air in the direction of a thorny lime tree. The cat meowed ferociously, hissed at the tree, fought with the leaves, and scratched the limes as it descended from what must have been the worst day of its nine lives. We never saw *misu* again.

The wildest thing Gabriel ever did at our house in Hato Mayor happened after what must have been a big dinner. He went into the front yard, squatted over a plantain leaf, and dropped a tiny turd. Without missing a beat, he flung it at Papá Victor, who was peacefully swinging in his hammock, puffing on his pipe. Thinking Gabriel had thrown a rock, Papá Victor shouted, *"¡Coño! ¡Muchacho de mierda, no tires piedras!"*[80] His exclamation, both unwitting and oddly prescient, sent Gabriel running for cover. When Papá picked up the "rock," he quickly realized what it really was—and promptly the switch came down on Gabriel's bare back.

Our neighborhood friends were pranksters too. It seemed like the only cure for the everyday boredom of our lives. Gabriel and I loved pranks the most, while Rony preferred to stay on the sidelines, opting for safer fun. The true master prankster, however, was my friend Ivan, who lived across the street. Gabriel and I learned this the hard way, through experience.

Ivan's family often traveled to New York, and he had two older sisters. He was a small boy with big eyes and an even

---

[79] Look!

[80] Fuck! You little shit! Don't throw rocks!

bigger mouth. He could talk his way out of anything, maybe even a death sentence. His pranks were creative, using whatever odd items he could find. Next door to his house lived a carpenter named William, who worked outside every day with an electric saw you could hear from blocks away. After each job, William would dump huge piles of sawdust in a corner of his yard.

Being the inventive prankster he was, Ivan decided to turn that sawdust into something mischievous. He made two *tortas* for Gabriel and me, using only sawdust and water.[81] I remember how excited he was to deliver them. His mother, Rosa, might have been in on the prank because I recall her smiling from the second-floor window as her little Dennis-the-Menace son darted out the door toward us. Her grin erased any suspicion I might have had.

"*Hola, muchachos! Hice dos tortas para ustedes,*" he said with his giant smile.[82]

We both bit into the dry sawdust, waiting for the sugary taste of cake to register, but were sorely disappointed. We spit the wood cake out as Ivan ran home, laughing so hard he cried tears into his gaping mouth. We cried too, with hatred and shame.

We didn't expect such a premeditated prank. The things Gabriel and I pulled off were always quick, spur-of-the-moment tricks that didn't require much planning or practice. After the *torta* incident, we were determined to get back at Ivan. My grandparents, on the other hand, thought it was

---

[81] Pies.

[82] Hi, guys! I made these two cakes for you.

hilarious. We, the victims, were the only ones who didn't find the joke funny. We needed to come up with something clever, something Ivan wouldn't expect. The plan came to me while I was sitting on Mamá Flora's rocking chair, watching an Indiana Jones movie dubbed in Spanish. That's when it hit me. We needed to set a booby trap for Ivan.

I ran to Gabriel with the plan, and he loved it. We used our environment to beat him at his own game. William's vacant lot was a perfect place for the setup. We gathered a couple of cardboard boxes and dug a pit in William's lot. We made sure Ivan was not around. We dug a hole as deep as we could. It must have taken us three hours to dig the hole large enough for a six-year-old boy to fit in, at least halfway. We thought about going to the riverbed near the tobacco factory to collect small crabs to deposit in our pit, but that required more work on our part, and we were not sure about catching anything.

Instead, we settled for smaller, more compact crawlers. The fire ants that decorated our front lawn again became useful. As they congregated around their sandy, mini-volcanic pyramid, we collected them with branches and ran quickly across the street, some of them falling on our bare feet, biting and making the mission more difficult. But it was all worth it. We deposited the angry devils inside the hole, as many as we could.

Then we covered the ant infested pit with thin layers of cardboard and scattered dirt to cover up our trap. Then we waited. The evening was approaching, and Ivan was soon to be home. Vengefully, we wanted him to think, if only for a second, that he was falling into the devil's mouth or to the other side of the world.

The plan was simple: Gabriel and I would pretend to play near the pit on William's property, luring Ivan over without raising suspicion.

When he got home, we made sure to act natural, rummaging through William's equipment like curious kids.

"*¡Hola, muchachos!*" Ivan called out, cheerful as ever. [83]

I responded casually, "Hey, Ivan, where've you been?" All part of the setup.

"*Con mi padre*," he said.[84]

To pull off our plan, I had to do two things: guide Ivan toward the pit without arousing suspicion and make sure he didn't see Gabriel's face, which was barely holding back laughter. Somehow, I managed both. Ivan strolled right toward the trap. The moment he reached the hole, he tripped and fell—face-first into the ground, not in the way that makes you laugh, but in the way that makes you wince.

At first, he cried from the fall, unaware of the ants swarming beneath him. But soon, he felt their stings, and the real pain began. The ants, furious after being kidnapped and thrown into that hole, unleashed their vengeance. Poor Ivan screamed in agony, while Gabriel, completely ignoring him, laughed uncontrollably.

Ivan's knees were scraped and bloody, and blood trickled down his legs, mingling with the dirt on his shins. Some of the ants mixed in with the blood, surfing over hemoglobin waves as he sobbed too hard to even swat them away.

---

[83] Hi, guys!

[84] With Papi.

Eventually, Ivan's cries summoned his mother, who came rushing down, screaming at Gabriel and me as if we were her own kids.

Ivan got his revenge when his mother stormed over to tell my grandparents what we had done. Mamá Flora didn't hesitate. She grabbed a branch from our guava tree and gave us a whipping we'd never forget, leaving us in our own puddles of tears.

But despite the pain, Gabrielito and I both agreed: it was worth every sting.

9

But all I hear is my own breathing and the blessed silence of those cool, clear nights under the anacahuita tree before any breaths a word of the future. And I see them all there in my memory . . .

Julia Alvarez[85]

I believe the mind stretches when we remember. Like a muscle, the mind must be trained to remember without pulling something out of place. I try to remember gently, in soft familiar movements—with compassion—listening to the cracks and aches remembering summons, how they make me feel. I offer those fleeting snaps of time to the imagination and give to you what comes.

After spending the first two years of my life in Jagua, our house in Hato Mayor felt like a castle, sprawling, almost like a maze you could get lost in. In the evenings, my family would gather in the living room to watch TV and pray the rosary. Sometimes we did both at the same time. Those nights made me feel safe.

With Papi traveling back and forth from the United States, having Mamá Flora and Papá Victor around was a comfort, even if all we did was sit together in front of the TV or pray. It was a peaceful time when things were good. And

---

[85] Julia Alvarez, *In the Time of the Butterflies* (1994).

for the most part, they were. Still, it seems that when times are good, we remember the little disturbances that break the harmony.

One summer, Papi came to visit us in the Dominican Republic. He had just finalized our travel papers, and Mami, Gabriel, and I would be heading to America with him that winter. I was six years old. On one of those summer nights, Mamá Flora pinched her rosary beads, pressing each one gently between her fingers, moving closer and closer to the tiny Christ at the end; the rest of us joined in prayer. Papá Victor, Mami, and Papi murmured along softly in the background. If you grew up Catholic, you'll understand how monotonous and endless praying the rosary can feel, the repetition lulling you into a trance of boredom.

There we were, sitting in a circle, chanting verses of the "*Ave Maria*" as we took turns praying.[86] The chant felt like a tiresome song, sung by weary voices, but we had to follow along. Children were often excused from leading the prayer because we'd inevitably butcher the lines, which was probably considered a sin. Luckily for me, that meant I rarely had to take a turn. Gabriel certainly never did. Our job was to mumble along with the leader, or at least move our lips, pretending we were mumbling.

It was dark outside; the crickets chirped, and the dogs were fast asleep. Mamá Flora sat beside Papá Victor, while Mami was next to Papi. But that night, the adults would sing a very different song. As we neared the end of the rosary, something shattered the sacred energy in the room. Mami and

---

[86] Hail Mary.

Papi began hurling words at each other, words foreign to me at the time.

After the final "*Ave Maria*" came a loud, sharp "¡Hijo-e-la-gran-puta!"[87] The curse shot through the room like a gun blast, ringing in my ears. Papi fired back with his own barrage of vulgarities. Gabriel was four years old, and the fear in his eyes was unmistakable. His cry pierced the air from the corner of the room. In an instant, the rosary prayers stopped. Hands that once held beads were now needed elsewhere—pulling and pushing, trying to break up the chaos.

I learned something that night. My parents weren't always "together." They weren't always my parents. There was a time they were just strangers without love. Their fight had erupted out of nowhere, with no tension leading up to it, like an *aguacero* that forms from a clear sky.[88]

The war of words quickly escalated into physical violence. Mami slapped Papi, and he reacted, shoving her against the wall, pressing her shoulders with a rage I hadn't seen before. My grandparents rushed to pull them apart—hands gripping arms, separating nails from skin—but it was futile. They fought like *gallos*, pecking at each other's throats, dragging their struggle into the bedroom.[89] Papi locked the door, and from the other side, all we could hear was Mami's voice, crying and yelling, louder and more desperate.

---

[87] Son of a bitch!

[88] Rainfall.

[89] Roosters.

Papá Victor held me close as the sounds of the fight intensified—objects thrown, glass shattering, the crash of a mirror, and then the sharp clank of metal. Silence followed.

Suddenly, Papi flung the door open and stormed to the kitchen. I slipped from Papá Victor's grasp and followed. Papi opened a drawer and grabbed a knife. He turned and headed back to the bedroom where Mami was still quiet.

Just before he reached the door, Papá Victor asked calmly, "*Y pa' qué e' eso?*"[90] I echoed the question, my voice trembling with fear. Papi's eyes were filled with hate as he replied, "It's to tighten a screw in the bedframe."

"Julito!" my grandfather shouted. "*Tu va' asustar ese muchacho!*"[91] Papá Victor held out his hand for the knife, and after a tense moment, Papi handed it over and stormed out of the house.

The next morning, I saw Mami. Her skin was a canvas of bruises—purple, blue, and yellow, like the colors of a nebula. We left for America that November, and I never spoke to my parents about that night again.

---

[90] What is that for?

[91] Julito! You're going to scare that child.

10

¡Dominicano hasta la tambora!

Every single Dominican, ever[92]

After we moved to Brooklyn, we returned to the DR every summer. But as I grew older, the trips began to lose their charm. I no longer felt the same connection to Jagua and Hato Mayor. By then, East New York, Brooklyn had shaped me into a shy, anxious, and bitter teenager.

The summer I turned fourteen was my last year in bilingual classes. I was starting to outgrow my Spanish. Traveling back to the DR meant putting my English away for the summer and dusting off the childlike Spanish that had taken a backseat. It's frustrating when you can't fully express yourself, and I felt stuck between two incomplete languages— neither English nor Spanish felt fully mine.

That summer, we went back to Hato Mayor, and I spent most of my time with Mamá Flora and Papá Victor. Occasionally, I'd hang out with Rony when he was around, but things were different. At seventeen, Rony was already married and a son to take care of, while I was still obsessed

---

[92] Dominican proverb that translates to "Dominican to the drum," implying that one is Dominican to max, Dominican to the utmost.

with PlayStation and Pokémon cards. Rony had outgrown our friendship, and I no longer fit into his world.

That was also the summer I earned the nickname "the devil of La Yagüita de Pastor." Let me explain. One day, we visited Mamá Carmita in La Yagüita, where she had been living with my aunts and uncles for several years. I usually looked forward to visiting them because I got to hang out with my cousins, Teresa, Fernando, and Magdalena. We arrived early and settled into our usual spots—kids in one room, adults in the living room.

Gabriel and I spent the afternoon with Fernando, who had a Super Nintendo. His room was in the back, almost completely separate from the rest of the house. Fernando was a few years older and never let us take a turn on the Nintendo. That day was no different.

"*Fernando, yo quiero jugar Nintendo*," Gabriel pleaded.[93]

"*No, muchacho! Tu no sabe' jugar esto,*" Fernando replied.[94]

To me, it felt like Frenando was getting a kick out of seeing us ask for a turn, knowing he won't let us have one. We were his audience. He was a skilled gamer, going through every level as if he had done it many times. Gabriel got tired of watching and went off to play with our little cousin, Raul. I felt like disappearing too, so I asked Fernando if I could take his bike around the block. I noticed his mountain bike as soon as I entered his bedroom. It was in good shape, covered in mud and dirt. It looked well-used and durable.

---

[93] Fernando, I want to play Nintendo.

[94] No, man! You don't know how to play this.

"*Está bien, cógela*," he said, but to make sure that I did not get it stolen.[95] Before walking out, he said "*ellos hay ladrones en e'to la'o. Ya tu sabe.*"[96]

"*Está bien, no te preocupes*" I said.[97] The last thing on my mind was robbers. All I wanted was to ride down the block. La Yagüita was a busy neighborhood with paved roads, full of life and movement. I took the bike out without bothering to ask Mami for permission. I figured if I could go to the park alone in Brooklyn, the same rules applied here. That bike felt larger than life. I could barely mount it and was terrified of tipping over before I even got going. The last thing I wanted was to embarrass myself, especially on Fernando's busy street.

The streets were alive with people, kids and adults everywhere. Some were listening to music, others playing dominoes or *vitilla*.[98] There were kids my age and older riding their bikes too, but the sight of large groups always made me uneasy, especially groups of kids. They looked suspicious to me, and the fear of getting jumped was always lurking in the back of my mind. That was Brooklyn's first real lesson to me: be wary of large unknown groups on blocks that aren't yours because you never know who's out to get you.

By then, I'd gotten jumped so many times that it was second nature to watch out for unknown groups of people, especially young people. I will never forget the first time I got

---

[95] It's all good. Take it.

[96] There are thieves around here. So, you know.

[97] It's all good. Don't worry.

[98] Street baseball.

jumped. It's not the pain that makes it memorable; it's the confusion, the fear.

It was in junior high, after school, at the jungle gym right outside. I remember my heart: the speed, the force, the tightness in my chest. I was on the monkey bars, watching a group of kids my age playing a game of "spider." One of them approached me and asked if I wanted to play. His face seemed friendly, his invitation kind. It felt good to make a new friend. But then, suddenly, that same kid pushed me to the ground. At first, I thought it was part of the game, my heart racing with excitement, not fear. Then the kicks started. They rained down on my back, my neck. Spit flew as they yelled slurs into the fading sunlight. Someone dragged me by my backpack. And all I could think was, *Why? Why are you doing this? What did I do? What can I do to make this stop?* And that's when your heart, that faithful *tambora* that's been with you since before your first breath, tells you: *you're in trouble.*

Deep down, I've always felt like a punk, a pussy, a coward and where I'm from, being a punk, a pussy, a coward is the worst thing a boy could be.

So there I was, on this too-big bike, wobbling down a street full of strangers. To them, I was just a new face. *el Americano* who couldn't even ride a bike properly.[99]

I kept riding down Fernando's street and explored a few nearby blocks. On my way back, I saw the neighborhood kids again. They were all biking together, laughing and joking. Mostly, they cursed: "*mamaguevo*" this and "*hijo de la gran*

---

[99] The American.

135

puta" that.[100] Dominican curse words are the best. They are more creative, and somehow funnier, than the ones in English. When I rode past them, they laughed hysterically, but without missing a beat, they looked toward me.

One of the boys called out, "*¿Tú eres el primo de Fernando?*"[101]

I nodded. They must have recognized Fernando's bike. They seemed interested in me and asked if I wanted to ride with them around the block. I was excited that these kids wanted to include me. As we rode, they asked me all sorts of questions about America: What language do people speak? Is it true that everyone is rich there? How tall are the buildings?

We circled the neighborhood a few times before stopping at an old house, just a couple of doors down from Fernando's. They told me this was where they bought *esquimalitos*.[102] The old lady who lived there came outside when she saw our bikes lined up in front of her property. She was wearing *calisos*, and balanced on her head was a large vaporous pot, chilled from the frozen *esquimalitos* inside.[103] There were guava, tamarind, passionfruit, and orange. I let the boys choose first, then picked guava for myself and paid for all our *esquimalitos*. I felt good about the day, the new friends, everything. I was even a little proud of myself. Making friends in East New York had always been hard for me. I was painfully withdrawn, but there, in DR, I seemed to be doing just fine.

---

[100] Cocksucker, son of a bitch.

[101] Are you Fernando's cousin?

[102] Dominican ices.

[103] Skippers.

After the *esquimalitos* woman retreated inside, something changed. The one who had been friendly toward me suddenly turned, calling me a "*mamaguevo!*" This time, there was no playfulness in his voice. I could see it in his eyes; he was dead serious. He wanted to fight. In my mind, he had already punched me, already embarrassed me, already made me the butt of the joke. My heart drummed, reminding me that it was happening again, telling me to prepare for what was coming. They were going to beat me up, just like I feared when I first laid eyes on them. I'd been here before. The boy tightened his fists, and my heart squeezed in my throat.

"*Tú crees que tú eres Dominicano?*" he sneered, glancing at the others before turning back to me with a maniacal laugh. Then, pointing at me, he spat, "*¿E'te tigre, dique Dominicano? Tú no ere' de aquí. Tú ere' un Americano come mierda.*" [104]

His spit landed on my face, refusing to slide off, stinging like his words, hitting me harder than any punch could.

I was never Dominican enough to be one of them. But if only they knew that in America, I didn't belong either. There, I was the kid in bilingual classes, the one monolingual kids pointed at and laughed at too. How could I explain that I didn't belong anywhere?

Before I realized how close he was, he slapped me, and my half-eaten *esquimalito* fell to the ground, melting on the old woman's gate. Another boy punched me in the stomach, and I stiffened. I couldn't move, let alone run for help. The sun felt brighter, more oppressive, as if it was on their side. One of them shouted something inaudible that felt like a spell,

---

[104] This cat, Dique Dominican? You aren't from here! You're an American shit-eater!

walking toward me with a menacing smile. I finally managed to get back on Fernando's bike, ready to escape. But just as I did, the leader grabbed the tire and pressed the valve, releasing the air. They howled with laughter as the tire hissed and deflated, leaving only the rim.

That's when something inside me snapped. I blacked out, an unknown force taking over me. The sun burned my forehead, and I was furious. Furious about the *esquimalito*, furious about the pesos I'd wasted on them, and furious at them, especially the leader. I dropped the bike and charged at him, ready to fight, ready to die for that air he let out of my tire. That air felt like mine: my pride, my breath, the very oxygen in my veins, and I wanted it back.

I grabbed his shirt, but he just laughed, as if my anger was a joke. His laughter enraged me even more. He wasn't fighting back, and that made me feel even smaller. Was I that pathetic, that even in my bravest, angriest moment, I was still someone to laugh at?

Through his laughter, he muttered, "*Fue Fernando... fue Fernando que no' mandó!*" [105]

The thought of Fernando behind this—laughing at me, orchestrating the whole thing—turned my rage into something darker. Fernando, my cousin, the one I trusted, had made these boys pretend to be my friends only to humiliate me. Suddenly, all my fury was redirected at him. Fernando became the puppet master of my shame, laughing through the mouths of these boys, his goons of torture.

---

[105] It was Fernando. It was Fernando who sent us!

I tore my eyes away from their laughing faces, left the bike by their dirt-covered sneakers, and ran straight to the source of my rage. Blinded by hate, I burst through the front door, past the living room where the adults sat reminiscing about the good ole days, maybe about life in the *campo* and their childhoods. My knuckles were clenched, my teeth grinding together. And then I saw him, in his bedroom, staring at the TV, the game paused, with Mario hovering over a pit of pixelated lava.

Without waiting for an answer, I demanded, "*¿Fuiste tú, Fernando? ¿Fuiste tú que les dijiste?*" [106]

I'm sure he saw the tears in my eyes, and he knew they weren't from physical pain but from betrayal. But he couldn't empathize with those kinds of tears. His eyes looked confused, but his smirk told a different story.

"*¿De qué estás hablando, muchacho?*" he returned. [107]

I couldn't hold back anymore. I charged at him, tackling him off the bed, hoping to pin him down and punch the smirk off his face. I wanted to land blows like fists of steel, but it never happened. He overpowered me easily, standing me up on the bed, holding my wrists together as if arresting me. His body felt like a wall I couldn't break through. I screamed in frustration, but that only made him laugh harder, a loud, gut-wrenching guffaw that burned me to the core.

No one in the house heard the commotion. This moment belonged only to me. Eventually, my little cousin, Raul, appeared. He must have been nearby. He stood at the door,

---

[106] Was it you, Fernando? Who told them to do this, was it you?

[107] What are you talking about, man?

unsure of what to make of the scene, me, yelling, and Fernando laughing.

"*¡Yo no fui!*" Fernando kept repeating, "*¡Yo no fui! Fue Magdalena, fue Magdalena,*" he said, still laughing, shamelessly blaming his older sister. [108]

I hesitated, my anger shifting yet again. Fernando had lit another flame, redirecting my fury. Now it was her I was after. He let go of me, satisfied, and I turned from him with Magdalena in my sights. It didn't really matter who I blamed. All I knew was that I was angry, and whoever caused that anger would have to answer.

I stormed out of Fernando's bedroom and retraced my steps through the front door, my face streaked with tears, hands curled into knots. My appearance interrupted the flow of nostalgic conversations in the living room, where the adults sipped their *café*, ruminating. They looked at me, baffled. One of my aunts asked what was wrong, but I couldn't answer. Outside, the sun was setting, and the stray dogs were yelping for scraps in front of Tío's house.

I rushed past the concerned faces and into the *galería*, where Magdalena was talking to a neighborhood boy she had a crush on. She towered over me, in her mid-twenties, and didn't seem to notice my heavy breathing, or maybe she did, but didn't want me to interrupt her moment.

"*¿Fui'te tú, Magdalena? ¿Tú le dijiste a esos muchachos?*" I asked, my voice mechanical, barely finishing the sentence, and without really caring about her answer. [109] I only asked to seem

---

[108] It wasn't me! It wasn't me! It was Magdalena! It was Magdalena.

[109] Was it you, Magdalena, who told the boys to do it?

somewhat sane to the boy standing beside her, who looked at me like I had horns growing out of my head.

"*¿Fui'te tú?*" I repeated, this time louder.

Magdalena glanced at her crush, then at me, and replied with chilling calmness, "*Piérdase.*" [110]

If something had broken in my brain at the start of all this, it was now beyond repair, shattered into a million tiny pieces. Whether it was the last bit of fear or the final shred of dignity, it was gone. I had nothing left to lose. I was already a joke. Before I knew what I was doing, my fists curled into *escopetas.* [111] I fired my right hand, punching her hard in the left breast. I aimed my left fist at the other, but she dodged it, quick as lightning. The boy shoved me back, and I stumbled.

Overcome with shame and frustration, I let out a scream, my throat raw with *vergüenza.* I turned and ran back into the living room, where the adults stared at me blankly. [112] My lips felt glued shut. I couldn't speak.

"*¿Y qué e' muchacho?*" my uncle asked, more annoyed than concerned. [113]

I was making too much noise. Even the dogs agreed, barking as I bawled in frustration. My eyes reddened, my heart raced, and my vision narrowed. I was having a panic attack, but to the adults, it was something else, something unnatural, unholy. It was the kind of behavior that made dogs bark and

---

[110] Get lost.

[111] Shotguns.

[112] Shame.

[113] What is it, child?

howl. And as everyone knows, animals can always sense when demons are near.

I screamed again, letting my anger take control, punching the wall until my knuckles bled. Fernando stormed in and tackled me to the floor, and we wrestled in a frenzy for a while.

The adults looked on, confused. "*Pero! ¿Qué es lo que tiene ese muchacho? Parece que tiene el diablo montado encima. Mírale los ojos, rojito como el infierno. ¡Habla, muchacho, qué es?*" [114]

When I couldn't explain my rage, they drew their own conclusions. Not understanding anger or frustration this intense, they turned to religion for answers. In no time, I was labeled possessed by *Satanás*.[115] My younger cousins, along with Gabriel, believed whatever the adults believed, so they too were convinced I was possessed. Films like *The Exorcist* had made this scene familiar to all of us. They'd all agreed I was in the early stages of possession. My skin wasn't blistered or pale from the coldness of the demon, and my head wasn't spinning around just yet. But still, they believed.

Faced with their diagnosis, I embraced it. Out of both anger and confusion, I decided to act like a possessed person. In a deep growling voice, I mumbled diabolical sounding nonsense, mostly English, Spanish, and Spanglish curse words: motherfucking bitches, *hijo de la gran* bitch, bitch-ass *yegua, samaran biche*.[116] I wasn't mad at any one person. I was mad at everything, at my situation, at who I was. My little cousin, Raul, either out of fear or bravado, took off his shoe and threw

---

[114] But, what is wrong with this kid? It seems that he has the devil over him. Look at his eyes, bright red like Hell. Speak, child, what is it?

[115] Satan.

[116] Son of a grand, mare, a Dominicanized version of son of a bitch.

it at me, just missing my head. I turned to retaliate, but before I could reach him, he bolted and locked himself in a bedroom nearby.

The adults, meanwhile, sat back without much reaction. They were simply witnesses now, an audience to a bad play.

I felt completely alone, as if no one else was there. And no one made any effort to stop me. I turned away from the living room and headed toward the kitchen. Someone shouted something about knives being sharp enough to kill, but I ignored them. I glanced at my family, then at the drawer of utensils, and opened it. Instead of grabbing a knife, I started bending my aunt's spoons into perfect U-shapes.

To them, this confirmed everything. They were sure I was lost in the darkness, a protégé of Lucifer himself, flesh and fire incarnate. At least, that's the story they told, and one I believed for a long time. In reality, I was just mimicking what I'd seen in movies, acting out my anger the way I thought the devil was supposed to. After bending a dozen spoons into U's, I threw a few on the floor and left the rest in the sink. To my family, these were demonic acts, and that's all they remembered.

From that day forward, I became the *poseído of La Yagüita de Pastor.* [117]

---

[117] The possessed.

11

I was still hearing explosions, which made me wonder whether the active shooter, or shooters, might not also be snipers who could be waiting to pick off those fleeing from the many stores surrounding us. I spotted a bush on the side of the parking structure and took cover there.

Edwidge Danticat[118]

After my episode, *dique, con el diablo*, I did not return to the Dominican Republic with my family again.[119] I spent my summers in East New York, where I felt more and more at home.

Growing up in East New York wasn't easy, but it wasn't the worst thing either. Whether I was heading to the corner bodega or walking to school, I always had to watch my back. I didn't know what it felt like to live in a place where you felt safe all the time, that only seemed to happen to white people in movies. My world was about staying on your toes, making sure you didn't get robbed on a dark street, jumped on the wrong block, arrested by a racist cop, or hit by a stray bullet.

---

[118] Edwidge Danticat, *We're Alone: Essays* (2024).

[119] With the devil.

When I moved from Brooklyn to Ohio for grad school, I realized my East New York paranoia had traveled with me. I'd catch myself closing the curtains of my apartment overlooking a quiet suburban street, thinking, *Someone could shoot me through the window right now.* I'd imagine my head exploding, brain matter splattering across the living room, and Mami crying at my funeral. Today, there are times when I look out a window, admiring the sun on the swaying leaves, and for a moment, bullets don't cross my mind. I know I've healed a great deal, but the terror still tugs at me now and then.

Things went down on my block. It wasn't like there was a *tiroteo* every day, but I witnessed enough violence to last a lifetime.[120] I'm not trying to reflect on these moments with some deep revelation, because the truth is, everyone experiences violence in one form or another, whether they live in the hood or not. And everyone processes it differently. We all learn from the pain, whether we're the ones who suffer it or witness it or straight up inflict it. My focus here is on how those moments of violence shape the writing I want to do, how my experiences in the hood, one of countless others, inform my perspective.

But let me be clear: the "hood" I'm talking about is the East New York, Brooklyn of my childhood, not the Brooklyn that's been rebranded in the last decade as the hipster capital of the world.

Any reflection about violence in East New York should begin with the acknowledgement that there's always been love in East New York, especially the East New York of my childhood. For all the crime and violence that surrounded

---

[120] Shooting/gunfight.

145

some neighborhoods, there was an equal amount of love and community. But it was still the hood. Some sold crack on the block; others smoked it. Some got shot; others did the shooting. I remember these moments vividly; how could I not? You don't forget someone smoking crack right in front of you, or seeing someone get shot on your way to school. That kind of stuff stays with you, no matter how much the neighborhood changes, no matter how many coffee shops pop up down the block. As both a victim and a witness to gun violence, those moments of fear became a crucial part of my adolescence.

The summer of 2003 stands out most. I was sixteen, and I thought I was the shit, a know-it-all who didn't know much at all but still felt like the world revolved around me. I was book smart but kept that hidden, like a bad haircut or a pair of fake Jordans. It was the middle of July, and Carlos, Pablo, Bart, Gabriel, and I were cooling off inside with the air conditioner. We were talking about basketball, as usual, replaying the game we'd just finished. I had lost to Carlos, who was a better player and wouldn't let me hear the end of it.

"You got lucky, son! No way you could beat me again. I bet whatever you want, you won't win another game," I said.

Carlos grinned and replied, "Yeah, aight. Just take your loss like a man and admit I'm the better baller."

Before I could come back with a response, we heard people running through the building's lobby and out the front door. Instinctively, we jumped up and ran outside to see what all the commotion was about.

Pablo's mother was out on the four-step stoop with the rest of *las vecinas*, and you know if *las vecinas* were gathered, something was going down.[121] They were chattering away—some in Spanish, some in English, and others in Spanglish—about something I couldn't quite make out at first. It wasn't until I saw it for myself that I understood what was happening. It involved my friend Stephen, a Puerto Rican cat with a wicked jump shot, about five years older than me, who lived down the block.

Stephen was pacing back and forth, shouting, and from the way he moved, I knew something was up. When he started pacing like that, it usually meant a fight was brewing. Once he was riled up, there was no calming him down. Stephen charged toward someone we couldn't see from the front of our building, so naturally, my friends and I sprinted down the block to get a closer look. The neighbors yelled after us in all kinds of languages: "Don't go! Stay out of trouble!" But we pretended not to hear them.

By the time we reached the end of Sunnyside Avenue, Stephen and Mohammed were already going at it, swinging wildly like untrained boxers. Mohammed was Stephen's best friend, both were inseparable, always playing on the same team, so this didn't make sense to us. They were tangled together, arms flailing, bodies crashing into each other in a chaotic display of strength. The fight spilled from Sunnyside onto Miller Avenue, right near Stephen's mother's house. It was a mess, two bodies tripping and crashing into each other, with no clear winner in sight.

By now, they were practically in front of Stephen's house. The commotion must have caught the attention of Stephen's brothers, Neil and Earl, because they came running outside,

---

[121] Neighbors (female).

147

red-eyed and furious. As the door flew open, I caught a glimpse of their mother inside, sitting at the kitchen table, staring blankly, seemingly indifferent to the whole scene.

Mohammed, spotting the two angry brothers charging toward him, decided it was time to make his getaway. He bolted down the block and jumped into his car. His tires screeched as he sped off, blowing through a red light in his 1997 Q45, disappearing almost as quickly as the fight had started.

After Mohammed left, my friends and I finally got a chance to talk to Stephen and find out what had gone down. It felt like a post-fight interview, and in our eyes, Stephen was the clear winner. He wasn't shy about gloating, either. We genuinely wanted to know what had happened. These guys were really close, at least that's what we thought. To us, they were practically legends, some of the best ball players on our side of East New York. But even best friends fight, right?

I knew how friendships could be. Just because you spend a lot of time with someone doesn't mean they're your best friend. To outsiders, it might look that way, and sometimes you believe it yourself. But often, this kind of closeness is built on convenience, someone who's always around, a friend of proximity and familiarity. That kind of closeness can breed friction, turning into misunderstandings, resentment, or even hate. Was that what happened with Stephen and Mohammed?

It turned out, there was more to the story. Stephen told us he found out his girlfriend had been sleeping with Mohammed. Stephen was in love with her, even though she treated him terribly. Back then, you couldn't admit to being in love. It made you look soft. You had to pretend the girl you were with was just one of many. But Stephen and his girl were serious, and she broke his heart. And it wasn't just her. It was a double betrayal, two relationships shattered. Mohammed, the guy Stephen was supposed to trust, had betrayed him too.

We were still talking to Stephen when the screech of burning tires hit our ears and the smell of rubber filled the air. A car came tearing around the corner onto Stephen's street, interrupting his story and making our hearts race. It was Mohammed. We turned our heads toward the Q45 speeding straight at Stephen, where it suddenly stopped, engine idling. We were terrified. Stephen looked scared too, but he quickly pulled himself together. The confidence he had an hour earlier was only half there, still recharging, while Mohammed's rage was fully loaded and ready to strike. Stephen stepped toward the car, gearing up for another round. We hung back, walking a little behind Stephen, trying to get a better view.

"What's good? You came back for more, son?" Stephen called out, half-smiling, maybe to seem in control, or maybe to intimidate Mohammed, who stayed hidden behind the tinted windows.

Stephen began speed-walking toward it, with us trailing behind, six feet back and moving slower. Then, before anyone could react, the automatic window rolled down, and out came Mohammed's arm, holding a silver Glock. He gripped it by the black handle, waving it left and right for a moment before locking onto his target.

All I could see was the Glock, gleaming, blinding us with fear. Stephen turned to run, but before he could take a step, Mohammed squeezed the trigger. Pop! Pop! Pop! The gunshots exploded, freezing time. The sound was so powerful, it rang in our ears for what felt like eternity—a piercing, immutable force. It was the sound of death coming, a quick blow to everything alive. In the seconds that followed, I felt nothing, as if my organs had failed me. The car sped away in silence, and that was that.

Once the moment settled in, we all noticed Stephen on the pavement, bloody and in shock. To us, he was already a corpse. I felt around my chest to make sure I wasn't hit, to make sure I was still alive.

That day, we learned just how much blood the human body holds. Stephen kept gushing, and it felt like it would never stop. That was all you could see on the sidewalk: thick, red pools spreading across the curve, staining Stephen's shirt and pants, encircling his collapsed body. His brothers' hands and faces were covered in it as they lifted him off the ground, shouting and arguing about what to do. His little sister stood frozen, screaming in shock, thinking her brother was dead. I thought the same. There was so much blood, it was impossible to tell where it was all coming from.

Stephen's brothers hoisted him up, and someone opened the front door to his mother's house. There she was again, like a ghost, silent and still at the kitchen table, completely detached from the chaos. They carried Stephen's limp body past her, might as well have been through her. From my place on the street, I watched as they laid him out on the kitchen table and called for an ambulance. Later we would learn that Mohammed had shot Stephen in the thigh and then another time but missed.

The police arrived first, as expected, and started questioning everyone, including me. I didn't have much to tell them, and neither did my friends. But the *vecinas*, who had watched from a distance, had plenty to say. They gave the cops enough information to piece together a story, at least a logical one. To them, Stephen and Mohammed were just criminals, and that was all that mattered.

Blood was spilled everywhere in Brooklyn. If you didn't witness it, you might have been the one who got shot. I can't say Mohammed didn't know better. He did. He was soft-spoken, laid-back, the kind of guy who listened with his eyes and never hogged the ball on the court. But the hood has a way of teaching us the wrong lessons: how to fight or how to kill over what little dignity or truth we think belongs to us. It's a lesson designed to destroy us from within. That day, when Stephen bled out on his mother's kitchen table, we all bled with him. The whole block felt like criminals in the eyes of those cops.

My life today is a world away from the speeding bullets of my childhood, but gun violence hasn't gone anywhere. I may not worry about getting shot over a basketball game anymore, but I do worry about getting shot while shopping at Costco, or while watching a movie with my family in a theater. I worry about sending my daughter to school, wondering if I should buy her a bulletproof backpack so she can walk through bulletproof doors.

I think of December 2012 at Sandy Hook Elementary School in Newtown, Connecticut Sand, where 20 children and six adults were murdered in one of the deadliest school shootings in U.S. history. Those young, beautiful lives snuffed out in an act of war against our most innocent. Children who were just learning to love school, dressed in vibrant colors, some with missing teeth waiting for the tooth fairy that never came. They had favorite stuffed animals, soft and worn, in shades of pink and purple, like the colors of a dawn sky.

I live in fear of getting that phone call. Of watching another tragedy unfold on the news, as police in military gear stand outside, waiting—just waiting—while gunshots echo inside. I think of the 19 students and 2 teachers killed in the Uvalde school shooting on May 24, 2022, at Robb Elementary School in Uvalde, Texas. Those kids had names that flowed like music, names that could've belonged to my cousins, my daughter's future *tíos* and *tías*. Some of them were avid runners, winning field day races. One boy was excited to learn football plays from his grandfather. Another, just 10 years old, dreamed of becoming a lawyer. A girl had been saving for a trip to Disney World. Another had just celebrated making the honor roll with her family.

Gun violence in this country is an extension of the global war machine. Guns are part of the story, but not its whole. It's important to understand the bridge between a teenager who picks up his father's automatic rifle and opens fire on his classmates and a military drone that drops bombs over civilian homes. These acts are not disconnected. The wars between Israel and Hamas, Ukraine and Russia, and the ongoing tensions between Israel, the United States, and Iran reflect similar logics of violence. The gun and the bomb are not the last resort; they are the preferred exclamation marks of so-called diplomacy. Displacement, intimidation, silencing, death, these are their ends.

So it's no surprise to me when private citizens behave like their governments, picking up deadly weapons as the only solution to their problems, as the ultimate punishment of their perceived enemies.

Our justified outrage at the murder of small children—our own children—should extend to the war machines snatching the lives of civilians across the world. As I write these words, the Israel-Hamas war continues. The Gaza Health Ministry reported over 57,000 Palestinians killed in Gaza as of July 4, 2025, 70% of whom are women and children. Approximately 1,200 Israelis, mostly civilians—college students, elderly, and children—were killed in the October 7 attacks. These horrific numbers continue to grow. As I type these words, tiny fingers are buried under rubble, their hands crushed to dust beneath tons of debris. And our American tax dollars pay for the bullets and bombs that bury those sons and daughters, mothers and fathers.

We see the carnage on social media. We hear the cries. And yet, we are told to look away. Students across the country are risking their futures—grades, degrees, even expulsion—to practice their First Amendment rights. They are using their voices, often for the first time, to speak out for what they believe is just. They ask us to see. And what have they been met with? Surveillance, suppression, punishment.

Since the return of Trumpism—Trump 2.0—we've witnessed a wave of escalated state repression: students snatched off the streets by federal agents; others detained in ICE facilities for months without legal representation. Some have lost their student visas. Others, even U.S. permanent residents and citizens, have been barred from reentering the country. Many have been expelled. Many live in fear. And those are only the stories that made national headlines. What happened to us?

There is a growing belief on the right that the left "hates" America, that dissent is treason, that protestors are enemies of the state and undeserving of the inalienable rights promised by the Constitution. It is a McCarthy-era logic, resuscitated by fear, antagonism, and profound misunderstanding.

But the left does not hate America. The left is angry with America. And there's a difference. I always return to the words of James Baldwin, whom conservative intellectual William F. Buckley Jr. once called "the number-1 America hater."[122] That accusation echoes the rhetoric of today's political discourse, in which to criticize injustice is to be labeled an enemy of the state. Baldwin replied—not to Buckley, but to the country: "I love America more than any other country in the world and, exactly for this reason, I insist on the right to criticize her perpetually."[123]

That, I think, holds true for many Americans today—student activists and people in general—who raise their voices not out of contempt but out of care. Their example should be our guide: honest, critical engagement with our country's failures, not to tear it down, but to strengthen it. But that's not the example we're setting.

We are told we cannot criticize government overreach. We are told we cannot call out inhumane military operations that kill thousands. We are told we cannot say that Palestinian children should not be bombed. To make such statements is to be accused of "taking a side" in a centuries-old conflict. Furthermore, some supporters of Israel view any criticism of the military's actions, the Palestinian death toll, or the suffering in Gaza as a form of antisemitism. And while it is undeniable that in recent years there has been a rise in

---

[122] Sam Tanenhaus, "When William F. Buckley Jr. Met James Baldwin." *The Atlantic* (2025).
[123] James Baldwin, *Notes of a Native Son* (1955).

antisemitism around the US, saying Palestinians have a right to live does not deny Israelis that same right.

The history of the region is complex like the history of any region that has been colonized. It includes the ancient and modern ethnic makeup of both Arab Palestinians and Jewish people, stretching back millennia. It is a shared history of dispossession and forgetting.

On one side, as Rashid Khalidi argues in *The Hundred Years' War on Palestine*, a vast literature has tried to prove that before the advent of European Zionist colonization, Palestine was "barren, empty, and backward."[124] The West's modernization—military and cultural—offered little to Palestine, whose governance structures were fragmented and under-resourced before 1917. One of Khalidi's most important arguments is that colonization always attempts to rewrite or erase history: "The point being made is that the Palestinians did not exist, or were of no account, or did not deserve to inhabit the country they so sadly neglected."[125] Today, there are no fully functioning national historical libraries, historical societies, or universities in Gaza. Most have been destroyed or severely damaged.

On the other side, the Holocaust is inseparable from the history of the region—for good reason. Hitler's campaign to exterminate the Jewish people was a world-historic failure of humanity. So too is the campaign of extermination currently unfolding in Gaza. The world must stop failing this region. That means refusing to justify the thousands of

---

[124] Rashid Khalidi, *The Hundred Years' War on Palestine: A History of Settler Colonialism and Resistance, 1917–2017* (2020).
[125] Ibid.

murdered Israeli civilians. And it also means refusing to justify the more than 57,000 dead Palestinians. As Palestinian activist and writer Mohammed El-Kurd puts it in *Perfect Victims and the Politics of Appeal*: "[Palestinian] massacres are only interrupted by commercial breaks. Judges legalize them. Correspondents kill us with the passive voice… Israeli death is the main story."[126]

I am not an expert in the history of war or West Asia and North Africa. Some will say that should disqualify me from speaking. That's fair. But like millions of people around the world, I want to understand what drives this depravity. How we arrived here, in a world of guns, bombs, and silencing. Ta-Nehisi Coates, in *The Message*, writes: "In a place like [Palestine], your mind expands as the dark end of your imagination blooms, and you wonder if human depravity has any bottom at all, and if it does not, what hope is there for any of us?" Maybe human depravity has no bottom, in Gaza, in Nazi Germany, in Trujillo's Massacre River. But if there is no bottom, why do we keep digging? Why do we dig at all?

As a professor of ethnic literary studies and the Americas, as an immigrant academic, and as a visibly brown man with tenure, I carry a deep guilt for perpetuating a pernicious silence around Gaza. That silence has bred confusion and fear in my classroom. I see it in my students' faces after horrific headlines, how they disengage, intentionally, from professors who can lecture on the Civil War, Manifest Destiny, or the U.S. occupation of Haiti and the Dominican Republic, but who say nothing about the

---

[126] Mohammed El-Kurd, *Perfect Victims: And the Politics of Appeal* (2025).

ongoing efforts to remove, displace, or destroy lives. But more than earning credibility, even respect, what I yearn for is their trust: trust that they have a voice in my classroom; trust that we can debate openly and respectfully; trust that they are not alone in their grief, anger, or confusion.

As a father, I feel inarticulate. I don't yet know how I'll explain all this to my daughter. I don't know how I will tell her that we live in a country that values guns more than children? I don't know how I will tell her that the national anthem she pledges at school doesn't promise allegiance to all Americans equally? That there is a generation of Palestinian children—some still in the womb—who have been murdered by a state-sanctioned war machine, while the world shrugs and says, "It's complicated"? How do I ask her to still believe in a future that is just and true when so many are oppressed in the name of freedom? And most of all, how do I teach her to be fearless when I am constantly afraid? What good is fearlessness in the face of a gun?

Thankfully, Stephen survived the gunshot, and Mohammed was eventually arrested and convicted. But soon after all of this, I fell into a deep depression. To be honest, I don't know if "depression" is the right word for what I experienced. It was more like an endless fog, an existential staleness, a constant state of confusion and silence. But most of all, it was a type of anger. Anger for being in a constant state of precarity, anger towards the things I wish I never witnessed because they were festering inside, contaminating how I saw and reacted to the world. This anger, this depression, this exhaustion by life itself intensified in my late teenage years, and continues to pay regular visits today.

Elizabeth Wurtzel writes in *Prozac Nation* that "A human being can survive almost anything as long as she sees the end in sight. But depression is so insidious, and it compounds daily, that it's impossible to ever see the end."[127] There's comfort in knowing that pain and suffering will eventually end, that at some point, you'll feel relief. But what happens when you realize there is no end in sight? When the source of your depression—the fear of dying, whether by a gun or by a government—never goes away? What then?

My anger is a type of depression, I've recently learned. It's more than just a disease. It's a silent killer, a parasite that breathes for me. And with every breath it takes, I feel a little more dead inside. To make things worse, sometimes I don't even know where it comes from, who brought it into my life, or how it got inside. It's maddening to be trapped in that cycle, stuck in time, stuck inside myself with nowhere to go, just bouncing off the walls of my mind. I've been there, often without realizing it. I've been there while I was physically somewhere else: fighting with Mami, arguing with Papi, getting into it with my siblings, or even in the middle of street fights. Seeing my friend get shot didn't cause my anger, but it made it worse. It intensified the weight I carried. It possessed me. And if I'm being honest, it still does.

---

[127] Elizabeth Wurtzel, *Prozac Nation: Young and Depressed in America* (1994).

12

I imagine one of the reasons people cling to their hate so stubbornly is because they sense, once hate is gone, they will be forced to deal with pain.

James Baldwin[128]

Those hyphens on the road turn to em-dashes when the foot presses the pedal, and at night, when there is nothing but the little red lights ahead and blackness, we don't care for the hyphens. We look at the dashboard and don't notice the speed limit. We look at our friends asleep and grip the wheel tighter as we dream of getting there.

My life changed the day I got accepted to graduate school. I had applied to twenty-three programs across the country, aiming high with schools like Harvard, Yale, and Columbia. I was ambitious, but as the weeks passed with no response, I started to lose hope. I was left waiting, wondering if any offer would come at all. Just when I was on the verge of giving up, I got the call: "We'd like to offer you acceptance . . ." It was happening. Suddenly, it wasn't too late for me to become someone I could be proud of. This was my second chance.

At the time, I didn't know what I'd do with a PhD in English, but I knew I wanted to spend my twenties immersed

---

[128] James Baldwin, *Notes of a Native Son* (1955).

in reading, writing, and honing my craft as a thinker, writer, and teacher. As soon as I got the news, I called Mami. I tried to explain that I was going to be a doctor, not the kind that heals bodies, but the kind that writes books and works at a fancy university. Let's just say that I left us both confused after that conversation. She didn't get it, but she could hear the joy in my voice, and that was enough for her.

In the weeks after my acceptance, I started feeling remorseful about leaving the hood, my friends, and my family behind. The excitement was mixed with a sense of abandonment, as if chasing my dream meant leaving a part of myself behind.

After I accepted the offer from Ohio State, a nine-hour drive from home, a strange sense of survivor's guilt set in. The weight of my final undergraduate semester, the stress of grad school applications, and the shock of receiving that acceptance letter all collided at once. I had worked hard for this moment, but when it finally came, panic set in. Was this the right choice? Moving to Ohio—a place I had never been, where I had no roots—was it worth leaving behind my community, the only place I truly felt I belonged?

In many ways, I'm still grappling with those questions. Leaving home, that sense of fitting in, changes how you see yourself—or how you fail to see yourself. Even my name shifted outside New York City. The rich, intricate sounds of my Spanish name were flattened by the English language. I was renamed, and I accepted it, all the while thinking: *it's okay, this is temporary. Let them have this version of me. My real self, my name, is waiting for me at home.*

I had to tell the block I was leaving, that I was moving to a place called Ohio. That day, I made the coffee extra strong.

The percolator gargled and then sang its usual tune, and the scent of coffee filled the room, grounding me in the moment. I poured myself a cup, added a little milk, sugar, nutmeg, and sat down on my sofa, the only piece of furniture in my living room. I opened David Leeming's biography of James Baldwin and started to read. What I loved most about that book was how it captured Baldwin's friendships, connections he formed with people like Bertice Reading and Engin Cezzar in Istanbul, Bernard Hassell in Saint-Paul-de-Vence, Beauford Delaney in Paris and Greenwich Village, Mary Painter in Bowling Green, Ohio, and Maya Angelou in Amherst. These relationships were beautifully described in words, but also captured in the black-and-white photos in the middle of the book, a little visual surprise that invited you into Jimmy's big, smiling soul.

I knew my friends would be outside, hanging around, waiting to see what the day would bring. Before I even reached the front door, I could already hear their voices. They were all out on the stoop—Gabriel, Bart, and Pablo—talking excitedly about something I couldn't quite make out.

My childhood friends are family. It didn't matter that they dropped out of high school, sold drugs, or did time. Their paths were different, and I respected that. We didn't share the same values, but we understood each other. They knew how much getting into grad school meant to me, and in their own way, they were proud.

"What's up, my dudes?" I said. "I got some news."

"Oh, word? You got it?" Pablo asked.

I nodded.

"I knew it! I told you, bro. Look at you, getting out of the hood. Just don't forget where you come from when you're around all them white people," he smirked.

"We gotta celebrate! Let's have a barbecue," Bart suggested.

Gabriel chimed in, "Yeah, hot dogs, burgers, beers. I'll set up the grill," referring to the bodega-bought portable coal grill that we used on the side-walk.

It was still early, and the coffee was kicking in. I gently chewed on specks of nutmeg to break the flavor. We didn't talk about me leaving after that. Instead, we just got into the day. Under the sun, with the air still cool, we grilled, drank beers, and shared stories: shenanigans of the club, money spent on drinks, street drama, and affairs. When Gabriel and Bart were around, a blunt was always being rolled. No words needed; one minute they were talking, the next they were passing the iron.

That night, as I stood in front of the mirror shaving, the guilt crept back in. Maybe it was the feel of the razor on my skin, or the quiet solitude of the moment. The person staring back at me, delicately shaving, was trying to tell me something with his eyes, a story I already knew. His gaze took me back, not so long ago, to the block. I saw myself as a kid, the new young'un on the corner. I saw Bart, Pablo, and then Ñaño and Broder, my first real friends. I saw our bikes resting by the stoop, our shins carved with scabs from scrapes on the concrete. I remembered the parties Ñaño and Broder's parents threw with their huge, warm Ecuadorian family, always welcoming us kids from the hood, our stomachs barking for a burger and a soda.

And then, in the mirror, I saw an innocent Gabriel, maybe ten or eleven, begging me to finish that level in *Tomb Raider* like the world depended on it, as if, in the end, we'd be rewarded for our bravery. That young innocent Gabriel slowly gave way to the grown-up version staring back at me, sweaty, wrinkled, his body trembling for the next high, the next hit. The story in the mirror wasn't just mine. It was ours. It was about the block, the brotherhood we'd built.

The guilt was simple. It was the fact that I have seen younger boys grow up to look older than me. Kids I taught to skate and play basketball dropped out of school to sell drugs, to walk the streets aimlessly looking for something to do, someone to do, as if their lives were not enough, as if they were missing something that for some reason I had. *Me, but why me? Why not them? Why not my friends? Why not my brother? What did I do to deserve a second chance at life?*

I looked in the mirror again as the blade approached the left side of my chin, and I saw my sixteen-year-old self. He told me that I turned my back on the hood, that there were sixteen-year-olds like me running around, and they needed me here. This hit me hard. It felt true. The guys outside needed me, I kept thinking, but it was exhausting to build from the bottom up without any help. I felt powerless.

I saw my eighteen-year-old self, and he asked me if life in Brooklyn was not good enough.

You have everything you could ever want here, a sick-ass apartment, a job, family and your boys, why go so far to do something you could do here?

My hand trembled at his last remark as I dug the blade into the surface of my skin. A little blood ran down my chin.

Next, my twenty-one-year-old self said to me that *that* was the blood of my brother and sister running down, going to waste, the blood of the hood washing away.

Why go if you'll fail?" he continued. *What makes you think you can complete a PhD in a language that isn't yours, in a country that never wanted you? And if you make it, who will you become? And if you come out of it, will you ever return to where you know you belong?*

In the days leading to my move to Columbus, I thought about Papi's journey to the States. I wouldn't be pursuing a PhD in English if it weren't for his rite of passage to America. He left Jagua without knowing what to expect from this new place. In many ways, Papi took a risk despite immense fear. Now it was my turn. This move would test whether I had it in me, to leave, to endure, to become.

13

Passion is never enough; neither is skill. But try. For our sake and yours forget your name in the street; tell us what the world has been to you in the dark places and in the light. Don't tell us what to believe, what to fear. Show us belief's wide skirt and the stitch that unravels fear's caul.

Toni Morrison[129]

Papi was in my thoughts but so was a mixture of fear, excitement, and guilt at the thought of doing a PhD far from home. Those emotions, however, were all eclipsed by my unquenchable thirst for discovery, to grow as a person. I think Papi must have felt something similar when he first left the Dominican Republic.

It's a strange feeling, packing up your belongings for the first time, clearing away a space you've lived in your whole life, and loading everything into the back of a truck. I asked myself, "Where do I go from here?" I felt deracinated, pulled from my roots, yanked from the boiling energy of my home to be replanted in a distant place. It was disorienting and deeply heartbreaking. As I packed, I couldn't help but think about all

---

[129] Toni Morrison, "Nobel Prize Lecture" (1993)

the friends and families pushed out of Brooklyn, forced to move to Pennsylvania and New Jersey for lower rent.

I had applied to graduate programs in New York City, but they didn't want me. In a way, I felt pushed out by these institutions, just like the people leaving Brooklyn. These schools, whose bathrooms are cleaned by people from our community, wouldn't admit a Dominican immigrant. It's our people who keep the city running, who serve the professors their food and clean their homes.

Papi's restaurant job on 34th Street was just blocks away from some of the universities I dreamed of attending. I even mentioned this in my cover letters, hoping to point out a kind of progressive irony, a chance to represent. But life had other plans.

I remember Ñaño and Broder helping me pack the U-Haul, thinking, *holy crap, I have a ton of shit.* All my friends were outside, and while some of the less lazy ones helped carry boxes, the others contributed by talking, cracking jokes, and reminding me not to forget the hood. I couldn't have picked a better day to move. It was the kind of day made for picnics and BBQs. I felt a sense of relief as I finally started loading my life's belongings into the truck, out of sight. It was no longer just talk. I was really leaving East New York.

The best part was having Ñaño and Broder making the trip with me. This was going to be our first road trip together, and they were excited to see what Ohio was like. My other friends, meanwhile, reassured me that once I was settled, they'd visit me. But I knew they weren't serious. I knew they had their own lives to deal with. Gabriel, especially, was struggling with alcoholism, drug addiction, and depression, lost in his own world, and I couldn't pull him out. My guilt about leaving him was the heaviest. It eventually hardened into a kind of anger—quiet, internalized, and aimed at myself. I was angry for abandoning him at his lowest point. Angry for not knowing how to help. *But I had to go,* I told myself. *This was my one shot. If I screwed it up, I knew the opportunity wouldn't come around again.*

There we all were, gathered on that familiar four-step stoop, some of us lifting and packing, others just hanging out and chatting. As much as I had struggled on Sunnyside, and as much as I was drowning financially, it was still home. I couldn't imagine living anywhere else, but if I wanted my life to change, I had to leave. I had to sacrifice my apartment, my comfort zone, to chase something bigger.

Leaving the place that had seen both the best and worst of me was surreal, and I didn't feel as emotional as I expected. I just let the day unfold, waiting for it to finally happen. What else could I do? If I'd over thought it, the stress of uprooting my life and starting over without a single familiar face might've crushed me. But I reminded myself of the good things that would come out of leaving: Mami would move back into the apartment with her then boyfriend, Ramiro, and Julissa. That made the decision a little easier.

Mami hardly waited for me to leave before she started planning to remodel the place. The apartment she was moving from was just a train stop away, but it was a nightmare, overrun with roaches, and the rent was barely affordable. Before leaving, I paid Mami a visit there to say goodbye. She made it hard to leave, made it appear as if I was going to die soon, as if I were a distant memory or spirit she wouldn't see again, as if she couldn't just pick the phone and call me.

On my walk to Sunnyside, I noticed a pair of kittens in a cage in a cluttered, run-down vacant lot next to a community garden. Their furry heads blended in with the junk so well, I almost missed them. But as soon as I spotted them, they seemed to sense me too, their eyes locking onto mine. They meowed, almost like they were praying for salvation, begging for their freedom. They purred and rubbed against the bars, licking the cage as if they were trying to reach out to me. Layers of separation stood between us. I saw them through a fence that divided the lot from the street; they saw me through the small birdcage that imprisoned them. I felt connected to them in a strange way, maybe because of our polarized differences: me, human, free, on my way to a new place; and them, cats, trapped, helpless, their voices muted by metal bars. I called animal services, but no one picked up. I looked around, no one noticed them, no one cared. I kept glancing back at them as I walked down the block, feeling a little more guilty than when I arrived.

When I got back to Sunnyside, I found Bart on the stoop. I could tell he had been drinking, maybe from the night before, maybe he started early.

"My boy's heading to Ohio. Don't forget your bros in Brooklyn," he said slightly slurring his words.

The truth is, how could I ever forget them? People who leave aren't the ones who forget. You carry it with you, the block, the laughter, the grief, the nicknames no one else calls you. Those are the things that stick.

If anything, it's more likely they'll forget me than I them. I've seen it happen: someone moves to another borough, another state, another country. Then they come back, hoping to resurrect something—childhood, belonging, the good ole days—but it's not there anymore. Not really. Time doesn't wait for sentiment. The hood moves on.

Pablo was there too, "making moves," as he liked to say. Others dropped by, curious, but unsurprisingly, hardly anyone helped us pack the truck. Pablo asked one of his custees to lend a hand, probably promising him a little baggie in return. The guy politely offered to help, but I told him we were good.

As the moment to leave drew closer, I felt like I was slowly disconnecting from Brooklyn, like the surrealism was giving way to reality. All my possessions were stashed in the U-Haul parked in front of my building: my amateur paintings, paperbacks, houseplants, furniture, clothes. It was strange to have everything I owned in a pile. It made me feel small, like anyone could just pick me up and drop me into whatever pocket of space they wished. In a way, that's exactly what was happening.

I could have ended up in Santa Barbara, Chicago, Cambridge, or nowhere at all. That's the thing about chance: it rarely announces itself, and it owes you no logic. In the end, the destination mattered less than the direction. What mattered to me was that I was chasing something that felt like mine.

The hood taught me that, not in words, but in what it cost to leave.

14

Perhaps this is how racism feels no matter the context—randomly the rules everyone else gets to play by no longer apply to you, and to call this out by calling out "I swear to God!" is to be called insane, crass, crazy. Bad sportsmanship.

Claudia Rankine[130]

We emerged from the Holland Tunnel, and as I looked toward the Freedom Tower from the other side of the Hudson, something about it felt right, like I was supposed to be there, inside a U-Haul with two of my best friends, heading to the Midwest. This wasn't Fitzgerald's city from the 59th Street Bridge. It was the city from across the river, from the continental side. It rose from the earth, monumental, as if it had always been there, a city for all cities.

The trip out of New York City was rough. The roads were bumpy, and the traffic was exactly what you'd expect. Brooklyn streets, in particular, felt like waves breaking at Jones Beach, rocking our U-Haul ship back and forth, causing our cargo to shift and rattle in the back. We thought leaving at

---

[130] Claudia Rankine, *Citizen: An American Lyric* (2014).

midnight would help us avoid the worst of it, and while there were fewer cars on the road, it was still New York City.

But we didn't mind. Ñaño took the wheel for the first leg of the trip, and Broder and I didn't object. Even though I had worked on a Tropicana truck for years and was probably the most familiar with trucks, I never actually drove one. Ñaño, though, adapted quickly, and once we left the city, the roads smoothed out.

Our first stop was at a TD Bank somewhere in New Jersey. Ñaño grabbed some cash, and Broder disappeared behind a bush to take a piss. We quickly learned that outside the city, everything is dark, so dark I still don't know how Broder didn't piss all over his leg. After that, we hit the road with no interest in stopping until we absolutely needed gas. We were eager to put Jersey behind us and push deep into Pennsylvania, that seemingly endless stretch of interstate. I sat on a milk crate in the middle of the cab. I played navigator, eyes glued to the GPS, reminding Ñaño when to switch lanes, when to exit, handing him water bottles as he drove. Ñaño had already decided he'd drive the whole 533 miles by himself. Broder stayed awake for most of the trip, but somewhere near Harrisburg, he dozed off, prepping for a shift that never came.

By 5:00 a.m., we were approaching Pittsburgh, another checkpoint for us. The anticipation of crossing into a new state kept us all alert. This was the farthest west we'd ever been. It was pitch black outside, and there wasn't much scenery to speak of, just eighteen-wheelers speeding past, making the U-Haul shudder. Every time they flew by, it felt like the truck was going to tip over.

Driving through Pennsylvania made me realize how little I actually knew about this country. I had expected the landscape to change, maybe to see mountains or lush forests, but instead, it was just endless stretches of road. When we finally hit West Virginia, the first hints of daylight began to appear. The amber glow of dawn leaked from the horizon, spilling into the fields and revealing the world that had been hidden in the dark: green pastures, farms, and old houses. It felt like an arrival, not just in distance, but in time. Though we were running behind schedule, we didn't care. Columbus was close now, and the GPS arrival time kept creeping later.

Ten miles outside of Columbus, we stopped at a gas station for coffee and fuel. The person at the counter looked at us like we were from another planet. With Ñaño's long cornrows, Hornets hat, and lensless 3-D glasses, and Broder's beard and tied-back hair, we must have been a strange sight to the sleepy Ohioan.

I didn't know it then, but I'd get many similar looks during my time in Ohio, confused stares from white people unsure of my existence. Those looks would sometimes morph into muffled insults about my appearance. Other times, they'd take the form of questions like "Where are you from?" or the dreaded "No, but where are you really from?" And then there were the simple euphemisms that cut just as deep, like "I know you're not from around here."

Even within the university, a place I thought would shelter me from such aggression, I was reminded of my outsider status. Once, a professor I deeply admired, someone whose research aligned with mine, told me after reading an essay, "If you want to make it in academia, you should always have a native speaker proofread your work." Her words were a punch to the gut, a brutal reminder that no matter how hard

I worked, my "not-being-from-here" would always stand in the way.

Another time, just before teaching a composition class, I went to a printing room, shared by faculty and graduate students. I found a well-respected scholar there, printing what I imagined were materials for their class. Not wanting to disturb them, I waited silently a good two or three feet away from the door. When they turned around and saw me standing there, their face twisted in shock, and they snapped, "Don't you ever do that again!" they shouted, storming off with a look of disgust. They were referring to my silence, to the fact that I stood there without announcing myself, without warning. As if my breathing, my waiting, my presence at the printer was a threat.

When Claudia Rankine's book *Citizen: An American Lyric* was first released in 2014, I didn't read it right away. Not knowing anything about Rankine's work, something about the word "citizen" kept me from cracking the book's pages. I was nearing my one-year anniversary of naturalization, so the word *citizen* hit too close to home for me. I once overheard a poet in my program say that the book captured the "subtle harms" of American racism. Reflecting on my time in this country and the Dominican Republic, I thought, *there ain't nothing subtle about that harm.*

But it wasn't that comment that kept me away from the book, nor the fact that I was shoulder-deep in the literature of nineteenth-century dead white men; it was this haunting word, *citizen.* The little encounters at the coffee shops with well-meaning and curious white people trying to find out where I was from, the professor's hand-on-my-shoulder advice about writing, and the shock and horror in the printing room, all were reminders that no matter what country I pledge allegiance to, I will never be wholly accepted. "Perhaps," Rankine writes, "this is how racism feels no matter the context."[131] What is racism, really, without all that it disembowels inside? And speaking up, Rankine's speaker claims, is "to be called insane, crass, crazy."[132] For me, I thought, "calling it out," was returning to the angry, ungrateful Dominican-Brooklyn immigrant I was desperately trying to run away from.

I kept those racist encounters with peers and professors to myself, too ashamed to share them with anyone. After all, I was one of the few immigrants in my department, and the only Latinx, Spanish speaker. I didn't want to give anyone a reason to think less of me than they already might have.

By the second semester, I grew to hate the parts of me that made me different from the other grad students: the way I sounded, my brown skin, even my natural Dominican baseball ass. I tried to iron out my Spanish and Brooklyn accents by reading aloud. I skipped meals to slim down. I avoided the sun to not tan my skin, hoping to look more like the ethnically ambiguous hipsters I despised back in Brooklyn.

I dated white girls in my program, seeking warmth in the arms and the prospect of *blanqueamiento*.[133] I always kept their race in mind, knowing deep down I could never be like them or, perhaps even be with them. I was careless with their

---

[131] Claudia Rankine, *Citizen: An American Lyric* (2014).

[132] Ibid.

[133] Blanqueamiento is the belief—passed down like a bad inheritance—that the closer you are to whiteness, the better your chances in life, love, and even history.

feelings, unable to trust their genuine care and affection, because I couldn't believe it was real. I'd convince myself they would leave me for someone else, someone better, because in my eyes, I wasn't enough. I was just a worthless Dominican immigrant, not white enough, not successful enough to be truly loved in a world that seemed to get whiter and whiter with each passing day. Even though this academic whiteness was new to me, there was something about it, perhaps it was the self-hate and the leaning into whiteness, that felt like something that had always been with me, even when I was a little kid in DR becoming aware of my skin color.

The internalized racism was killing me, and it was only my first year. To make things worse, nothing that I was reading was by people who looked, sounded or felt like me, that is until a couple of years into my grad program, I encountered María Elena Martínez's influential book *Genealogical Fictions* (2008) in the university library. As mentioned in chapter 6, Martínez charts the relationships between the Iberian peninsular cultural-religious concept of *limpieza de sangre* (purity of blood) and colonial caste systems in Spanish America, arguing that *limpieza de sangre* originated in medieval Castile, as a concept for the purity of Christian ancestry, distinguishing Jewish *conversos* (converts) and Muslims from a "pure" Christian group.[134]

I was obsessed with the connections Martínez makes between white supremacy and catholicism. By the sixteenth century, she posits, Spain became preoccupied with genealogical lineage and the purity of Christian ancestry which

---

[134] María Elena Martínez, *Genealogical Fictions: Limpieza de Sangre, Religion, and Gender in Colonial Mexico* (2008).

they believed made them more pious and purer. In Spanish America, a person's pure lineage became associated with one's Spanish ancestry and society, i.e., the closer you were to Spanishness the purer you were. Although the discourse of blood and lineage endured adaptations, by the colonial period, the concept of *limpieza de sangre* was still partly defined in religious terms, which had, according to Martínez, significant implications in shaping categories of identity, racial discourses, and communal ideologies. With strong religious connotations, the concept of *limpieza de sangre* became the basis for racial classification when transplanted to colonial America, contributing to the evolution of modern notions of race.

While in the U.S., the "one drop rule" system of white supremacy discouraged racial mixing, in Latin America, European colonizers promoted *mestizaje*: racial mixing between Spaniards and Indigenous groups, often eliminating the biological and cultural presence of African-descended people. This resulted in a complex hierarchical caste system of skin color known as casta, where white Europeans born in the continent were at the top and Black and Indigenous people at the bottom.

Martínez's text prompted me to think about my own subjectivity growing up in the Dominican Republic and the United States, the lack of anti-racist practice within my community and the familial silence around blackness.

My reckoning with my racial identity began when I was a boy in the Dominican Republic and continues today. Mamá Flora did not like to talk about her past. When I asked her about her father, she often mythologized his blackness as rumor and folklore.

She'd say, "There was a rumor that Papi's father was a Haitian man, but I never believed that."

For a long time, I wondered if she was ashamed of her father's race and ethnicity. I wanted to know where this shame and denial came from. Mamá Flora died before I could summon the courage and articulation to ask. Her denial and shame were not univocal or unique. When I went to other family members with the same question, they gave me similar abstracted answers: "Your great-great-grandfather had a sister who spoke Spanish with a heavily Haitian Kreyòl accent."

Mami was the opposite. Many saw her as a white woman. Family and friends affectionately called her, *la rubia*.[135] She never talked about blackness. Instead, I grew up hearing stories of my maternal Spanish great-great-grandmother who came aboard a steamer to the island, you know, the mythical Julia Álvarez of our family, who didn't, as far as I knew, write great books. We knew almost nothing about her, yet her story fed an intense marvel within me that I thought was mere curiosity. But it wasn't simply that. It was an idealization of the Spaniard; the whiteness that I often saw celebrated in our Dominican history, popular culture and community that made me want to know more about her.

No one seemed to deny being a *rubio/a or a blanco/a*, at least not like many denied being *negro/a, moreno/a, and Haitiano/a*. It seemed to me that regardless of the social context, being white was a compliment while being Black, in some contexts, bordered a slight. Deborah J. Yashar reminds us that after gaining independence, Latin American governments undertook nation-building projects that relied

---

[135] The blonde.

on national, cultural, and racial myths.[136] Such myths were shaping forces in how Latin American governments promoted racial harmony and erased ethnic differences from nation-building documents and discourses. Yashar argues that the "blurring of ethnic lines, sanctioned by governments, contributed to fluid understandings of race and identity. Whereas in the United States, anyone with mixed Black and white heritage was historically considered Black, Latin American societies developed various categories of racial identity based on skin color . . ."[137] The Latin American idealization of racial harmony made light skinned minorities less likely to ally themselves with Black Latinxs. Instead of fighting for the equal rights of Black and Indigenous people, many chose to lean into the myth of *mestizaje* because it afforded them higher social standing as the nation's ideal. I started becoming the very thing that was oppressing me.

That's around the time I started dating my now spouse, a Korean-American PhD student who was a year ahead of me, studying nineteenth-century Anglophone literature and Romantic poets. In a way, we were both immersing ourselves in the words of dead white men, trying to crack the very language that had tried to crack us. We shared a deep love for words—poetry and prose alike—along with a passion for fashion and art. But our upbringings couldn't have been more different. Her parents were both medical doctors. She grew up with three sisters in a household that went on cruises and international vacations, stayed in hotels, and regularly dined

[136] Deborah J. Yashar, "Does Race Matter in Latin America?" *Foreign Affairs* (2015).

[137] Yashar, "Does Race Matter in Latin America?"

out at restaurants. She often shared stories of being bullied in school for how she looked, interrogated about her origins, tested by complete strangers on her ability to speak English. Ohio in the 1990s, she said, reminded her constantly, in ways big and small, that she wasn't "American" like everyone else. But she was born in Chicago and raised in Youngstown, and I couldn't help but think: what could be more American than that? My partner's story resonated with mine, not in form, but in spirit. And through that shared recognition, that solidarity born of displacement, we found solid ground to walk on, to build a life.

When we met, I was struggling financially. My graduate student stipend barely covered rent and bills, leaving almost nothing for food. Most of my meals came from the local CVS: microwavable mashed potatoes and beef, a few packs of spicy peanuts, and the occasional honeybun. Sometimes I'd switch it up with a microwavable pizza or burrito. If I really wanted to splurge, I'd walk down High Street to the Chinese restaurant for a taste of my childhood comfort food, the beloved hood Chinese dishes I grew up on: pork fried rice, General Tso's chicken, boneless spare ribs, and always lots and lots of hot sauce.

At first, we were just good friends. I helped her through a messy breakup. After bad dates, she'd come over to vent, and we'd commiserate while I played reruns of *The Office* or *The Twilight Zone* in the background. Any romantic feelings I had for her, I convinced myself, weren't worth risking the friendship, one of the few genuine ones with someone who didn't need anything from me. Besides, I didn't think she'd want to take a chance on someone who had a reputation as a *mujeriego* and heartbreaker. I couldn't blame her. But things did progress, albeit slowly at first, and eventually, we decided to give *us* a try.

It was a hard truth to swallow, realizing that being a PhD student didn't protect me from poverty. I was still a broke Dominican immigrant, just in Ohio now.

The summer before my second year, I had to sublet my apartment. My partner took me in, like a stray she'd rescued from the streets. I packed my things again into a U-Haul and thought about the night I moved.

The night after Ñaño and Broder left for New York City, I felt alone. Having them around was like having a piece of East New York with me, a continuation of all the memories I had grown up with. So, when their blue cab pulled up, and I walked them both to the car, I could not help but wish I could go with them. They were my last link to East New York, and the sight of that cab pulling out, making that turn into the darkness, was heart-wrenching. I walked into my apartment and ugly cried myself to sleep. They were neutral tears, I told myself, tears that reminded me I was human and that those two guys were my family for life. *Tomorrow*, I kept telling myself, *will be better. Tomorrow will start to feel like home. Tomorrow . . . who knows anything about tomorrow?*

15

As we learn to bear the intimacy of scrutiny and to flourish within it, as we learn to use the products of that scrutiny for power within our living, those fears which rule our lives and form our silences begin to lose their control over us.

Audre Lorde[138]

The way I remember Lou is probably the way all his boys remember him. He'd roll up on his mountain bike or a BMX, with a thick beard and a big smile, towering over everyone at six feet tall. He was a tattooed Dominican kid who loved to have fun, whether biking around or smoking a blunt on the block. But more than that, Lou was someone you could count on, wise beyond his 21 years, even though a bad decision ended up costing him his life. The last time I saw him was the summer of 2013, just before I moved to Ohio.

It was the summer of drill music, but really, it was the summer of Chief Keef. *Raris and Rovers. That's that shit I don't like.* The sound of Chicago bleeding through broken car speakers and bootleg aux cords, sharp and smoky like something flammable. We played it loud, louder than we

---

[138] Audre Lorde, "Poetry is Not a Luxury" (1984).

needed, louder than the block could handle. The rhythm didn't just hit, it stomped.

We wanted to feel like Keef's Black Disciples (BD) in the music videos. The camera, always coming in and out of focus, caught it perfectly: steely faces, shiftless torsos, shoulders bouncing with the beat, heads nodding like they were keeping secrets. Fingers curled into gun signs, not in threat but in solidarity, tracing the music in the air while the room filled with weed smoke and spilled molly water, thick enough to baptize us.

That was the feeling then, twenty-something, broke but invincible, moving like the bassline was in our blood. Drill music was spreading throughout East New York before Pop Smoke and Fivio Foreign. It made the world feel sharper, more urgent, like every beat drop was a door kicked open. And Lou? Lou was the leader of it all. He had that look, that lean, that offhand swag, that Based God quality, like he'd invented the songs just by living.

When I got back to the block from Hunter, the usual crew was hanging in front of my building. Seeing them made me feel a little helpless, like we were stuck fulfilling some statistic, just standing around, smoking weed, drinking beer. I gave Carlos, Lou, and Bart each a pound. The outdoor lights kept flickering on and off, making it hard to even see their faces clearly. Lou had a New York Knicks hat pulled low over his eyes, a hoodie layered over it. Before I headed inside, he looked at me, his eyes tired and contemplative, and said, "Keep it one hundred, my G."

That was the last time I'd ever hear his voice.

The next morning, I woke up to a text from Gabriel around 7 a.m. It read: "Lou died last night."

I didn't understand. I threw on clothes and walked outside to see if anyone was around. The block was full: Bart, Carlos, and the others who were close to Lou. We stood there, silently looking at each other, searching for something to say that would make sense of it all, or at least reassure us that we were still here. We talked about Lou's like we didn't believe it yet, speculating what actually happened, when he would return.

As we talked, my upstairs neighbor Evan, one of Lou's closest friends, walked up with his dog Mojo, a pitbull nearly half his size. Mojo was a beast, terrifying to anyone who hadn't watched him grow from a pup. Evan looked at us and shook his head, and all knew that Lou wasn't coming back to us.

Evan had just come from Lou's mother's apartment. Lou's body was still lying on the bedroom floor without a heartbeat. Evan said he couldn't bring himself to even look at him from the doorway. "He OD'd," Evan said. "They saying it was K2."[139]

I could only imagine the sight, the weight of that senseless tragedy. Evan told us the hardest part was that they'd been hanging out just a few hours before Lou died. Lou had called him, but Evan, too tired, hadn't answered the phone.

We never confirmed the actual cause of Lou's death. There were rumors that he overdosed, mixing too many drugs at once. Some said he took a Molly and smoked K2, which

---

[139] K2 is a cheap, synthetic drug made to mimic marijuana, but it's unpredictable and often laced with chemicals that can cause psychosis, seizures, or death.

stopped his heart. When Lou died, it felt like the summer, all Brooklyn Based-God summers, died with him. A week later, we buried him. He looked at peace.

Sadly, Lou wasn't the only friend that we lost that summer. A month after Lou's passing, my friend Loso died in a catastrophic car accident. Loso was Gabriel's best friend. He was like a brother to us. The afternoon I learned about his death, I was sitting in a coffee shop working on grad school applications, and I suddenly noticed fifteen missed calls from Julissa and twenty from a number I didn't recognize. I somehow knew that number belonged to Gabriel who had a new number every other week. I returned Julissa's phone call and listened to her broken voice. Fatigued from crying, she said "Loso died last night in a car accident. He was on the news. Please call Gabriel"

I couldn't say much. Maybe, I was in shock. I turned back to my writing and tried to avoid processing any of it. I pretended I had never returned my sister's call and that I was still oblivious to Loso's death. I put on my headphones and Steel Pulse's "Wild Goose Chase" came on: "I thought the destruction / Of creation / Would be nuclear power / And radiation / I thought judgement / Would come / When dem drop / De neutron bomb."[140] To be honest, there wasn't much of a connection between the song and Loso's death, not at first. I wasn't searching for meaning. I was trying to distract myself. Trying not to think about him crashing his Honda Accord at full speed into the back of an MTA bus. The car folded in on itself, a crumpled line of steel and glass. The back of the bus split open like a peeled can.

---

[140] Steel Pulse, "Wild Goose Chase," *Earth Crisis* (1984).

I didn't expect it to hit me—but it did. Loso's death *was* our neutron bomb. Not in the literal sense, but in what it destroyed: the feeling of invincibility, the joy in our ordinary days, the belief that we had more time. His death made no sense. The radiation of his death ruptured something beautiful, something still in the making.

None of us who knew him closely ever really recovered. The last time I saw him, I was working in the back of the Tropicana truck on Fulton Street. He was shopping for something, maybe a fitted cap. He crept up behind me while I was moving boxes of half-gallon OJ and shouted, "Yo, what's poppin!" all teeth and laughter, like he was the good part of the day. And for a moment, he was.

"You scared me, son. I thought I was about to get robbed," I jokingly said.

I don't remember much of that conversation. But I recall that in the brief encounter we said a few words about our dreams. He wanted to be an airplane mechanic and was working on his GED. I wanted to be a writer, who did not have to work in the back of a juice truck. We took separate paths toward eternity.

Since I got that phone call, "Wild Goose Chase" has become a phonetic cue for the promise I made to my dead friend: a promise of persistence, resilience, diligence, and dedication to move forward with writing, even if moving forward hurts, even if moving forward will move me far from home, even if it kills me. I think about Loso often, the way he was, how animated, carefully dressed in the latest gear, cleanly shaven, perfect hairline, with a smile that could disarm the hardest and toughest. I think about what he meant to me and to my brother who loved and loves him still.

A lot of what I am doing here is scrutinizing how I grieve my friends. These were times of intense confusion, hopelessness in my crumbling world. Lorde says that when "we learn to bear the intimacy of scrutiny . . . those fears which rule our lives and form our silences begin to lose their control over us."[141] Even though Lorde was writing about poetry, I believe this is true for our lives too, when we scrutinize, we begin to heal. I know I've done some healing, but sometimes "the intimacy of scrutiny" peels open a scab that has not hardened, and "those fears" bleed out over me.

Loso's death weighed heavily on Gabriel. He became distant, draped in a fog of depression. The world was moving in mysterious ways, and none of us knew how to make sense of it.

Lou and Loso's deaths felt like tragedies you hear about from afar, things that happen to other people, things you feel sympathy for but don't fully understand. Then, suddenly, tragedy strikes your own life, tearing through your family, and you're left wondering: *Who's feeling sorry for me?*

It started to feel like my family was dying, piece by piece. And with death came distance. We were drifting further apart from one another. That's how I felt after Lou died, after Loso was gone, and after Gabriel slipped into his depression and leaned into drugs and alcohol. It was a growing void, one that I felt deeply as a person of color in academia, someone who didn't come from a stable or privileged background. I used to think I couldn't be more different from my family. But since

---

[141] Lorde, "Poetry is Not a Luxury" (1984).

then, I've learned that there's no limit to how far we can drift, how distant and different we can become, if we allow it.

Now, I refuse to let that distance grow even if it sets me back indefinitely. I'll work ten times harder to keep them close, to move forward with them by my side. Because once you lose touch with your family, you lose a part of yourself that's nearly impossible to recover. And I'm not willing to let that happen. I'm committed to them, in a spiritual way, bound by a blind faith I can't quite explain. Maybe it's because I spent so long trying to break away from what they represented, from who I thought they were.

I'm not sure what made me this way, but I know that the more I learn about myself and the world, the more I want to understand my family's lives—both the lives they've lived and the ones they could've had, had they been given the opportunities I have.

16

. . . no hallo un acento digno de ti.

¿Cómo tu afecto cantar al mundo,
grande, infinito, cual en sí es?
Me basta si te miro,

. . .

porque tu vista calma
los agudos tormentos de mi alma. [142]

Salomé Ureña de Henríquez

Mami was deeply religious, a true Catholic if ever there was one. A rosary-clutcher, a saint-worshipper, and a firm believer in the Holy Trinity. She once told me it was her essence to love Christ, that without this love, she wouldn't be the person she was. There's something admirable, even enviable, in knowing your essence so clearly.

---

[142] Salomé Ureña de Henríquez, "A Mi Madre," *Poesías* (1880).
I cannot find an accent worthy of you. / How does your affection sing to the world / which in itself is great, infinite? / It is enough if I look at you, / . . . / Because your sight calms / the sharp torments of my soul.

Mami was also the most superstitious person I've ever known. She found ways to make her three children, myself included, in the words of Michael Scott, "a little stitious," even if we never openly admitted it. Most of her superstitions revolved around death, little allegories of mortality. As strange and sinister as they were, they were effective. For one, they scared the hell out of us. And they worked because they made us behave.

As a boy, and even as a teenager, I had a bad habit of leaving my sneakers scattered all over the house: living room, kitchen, bathroom. Sometimes I made it worse by leaving one shoe in one room and the other somewhere else. You could often find me wandering around wearing just one shoe, searching for the other. It drove Mami crazy. As a housekeeper by trade, she spent her days cleaning other people's homes. The last thing she wanted was to come home to a messy apartment, sneakers strewn everywhere, her kids adding to the chaos she'd have to tidy up later.

Whenever she caught me with one shoe on, searching for the other, she'd say, "When boys walk around with only one shoe, their mother will die." Walking with one shoe was a sign, a curse we unknowingly cast upon her. Those words scared us to the core. It was an ominous thing for a child to hear, that something as small as wearing one shoe could bring death to their mother. That superstition stuck with me. Even now, when I catch myself walking around with one shoe on, I think of Mami's warning. And, if I'm being honest, it still unnerves me a little.

Another one of her death-related superstitions, which I later learned is common among Latines, involved dreams. Mami said that if you dream of broken or cracked teeth—

whether your own or someone else's—it's a sign of an impending death, either yours or someone close to you. That one never got as much traction as the shoe curse, mostly because I never had dreams about teeth. Ironically, after I moved to Columbus for graduate school, I started having those dreams, frequently. They were vivid and disturbingly real. In one, I'd be eating a sandwich, and as soon as I bit into it, my front teeth would crack or fall out. In others, my teeth would be lodged in the skin of an apple, sticking out like headstones.

Those nightmares made me brush my teeth more obsessively, but they didn't make me think about death, at least, not until I got some news from Mami.

In the fall of 2013, after I had left East New York for grad school, Mami began experiencing excruciating headaches; she also fainted regularly throughout the day. I never got to see her faint because I was already away, but Gabriel and Julissa told me that it started shortly after I moved to Columbus. I didn't know what to think and was still getting adjusted to a new town, figuring out how to be a graduate student and be productive with my study routines. I spoke to Mami about her symptoms.

Over the phone, she sounded very optimistic about the whole thing. She told me that she was sure it was nothing major and that the doctors were going to fix her right up. That was usually her answer to all her maladies, right before "*El Dios poderoso me va a sanar.*"[143] I repeatedly told her that God

---

[143] God Almighty will cure me.

would be there for her, but that for our sake, she should visit a medical professional about those headaches and more pressingly, her blackouts. I was becoming increasingly worried about what was happening. I was too far from home. I felt adrift, and this feeling was new to me. I found solace in my reading and writing, but the worry gnawed at me.

Hands Full of Silence

Today, in afternoon's hollow breath,
I taught Dugan's voice to a silent room,
and something rose like an *oración*.[144]

I learned as a boy that Mami and Papi
wore poverty like a room wears dust.

Mami swept strange floors,
the air sharp with bleach,
her body a sigh, her hands a prayer.

This is not a love song.
This is that rusted nail in the wall,
Mami scrubbing the cold dawn,
her breath pulling at the night.
There is no road back,

---

[144] Prayer.

only her steps in my dreams.
She crumbles on the floor,
her body scattering with the wind.

Papi's hands were made of stone,
his eyes two dark wells
with echoes of our becoming.

This is not a love song.
This is that cold grip of knowing
who you come from,
who taught you to survive.

For every lost word in her mouth,
I held one in mine.
I keep it warm in my chest.

17

Mami loves technology for the same reasons
She loves to call herself a resident and not a citizen
She wants to remember the staying more than the leaving.

Melania Luisa Marte[145]

One afternoon, Julissa told me, she came home from school and heard a thumping sound from the living room. Startled, she rushed in to find Mami on the floor, trying to regain consciousness, struggling to her feet after collapsing for no apparent reason. Julissa helped her up, and Mami, glassy-eyed and confused, looked at her in utter bewilderment and asked, "Who are you? Where am I?"

These episodes of temporary amnesia always followed her blackouts. Julissa recounted the story and others like it over the phone, her voice calm and reassuring, keeping me grounded as we spoke. But beneath my composure, I was terrified and guilty for being so far away, unable to help Mami and my siblings during such a frightening time. The fainting spells kept happening, and Mami held on to her religious

---

[145] Melania Luisa Marte, "Mami & Technology," *Plantains and Our Becoming: Poems* (2023).

optimism, refusing to acknowledge the severity of her condition.

Meanwhile, I was teaching my first undergraduate class and completing my first semester of graduate coursework. In the midst of it all, Mami, rather than seeing a doctor or getting a checkup, decided to travel to the Dominican Republic.

She had purchased a condo in Santiago in 2003 as an investment, thinking she might retire there one day. I spoke to her once while she was on the island. She sounded like her usual self, cheerful and happy to hear my voice. I asked her about the headaches and blackouts, hoping she would tell me they'd vanished after being back in the motherland. But they hadn't. She was still fainting regularly but seemed more accepting of it, more at ease with the idea of collapsing now that she was home, surrounded by family.

At first, I didn't see anything wrong with her trip. In fact, I thought being away from the States and reconnecting with family might lift her spirits and improve her health. But after we hung up, I realized how wrong I was. She'd never dealt with something like this before, persistent headaches and blackouts. It gnawed at me that something far worse than we could imagine was behind these symptoms. I tried not to think about it in the following weeks, burying myself in work, but the guilt festered. I felt selfish, more selfish than I'd ever felt in my life.

Work became my only escape. I worked until exhaustion took over, until my eyes couldn't stay open. But even then, I didn't feel like myself. I didn't feel like anyone. I couldn't recognize the person staring back at me in the mirror. My voice didn't feel like mine anymore. I was so far removed from the person I had been before moving to Columbus.

In Columbus, I could mask my pain, hide behind this new version of myself, far from the guilt and shame, far from the anger. No one knew me there. But retreating inward only made the remorse grow, thickening into something unbearable.

As the weeks passed, things only got worse.

A few weeks into my solitary and extreme study habits, I spoke to Mami again about her condition. She had finally gone to see a doctor, a few doctors for that matter, but was not given a straightforward diagnosis, so her condition was still a mystery to all of us. She kept her faith, however, and reassured me that all things were in the hands of *Dios y el Espíritu Santo*.[146] Hell! For the sake of her health, I hoped there was a God somewhere outside of her mind that would help us get through this and more importantly, restore her health.

Mami told me that she was scheduled for a CAT scan a week from that day. I saw the worst things in my mind, the worst outcomes, so with that in mind, I tried my best to keep moving forward with my studies, to distract the hell out of myself. I read more that week than I've ever read. Something inside of me told me I should not worry, that the thoughts racing through my head were not real, merely induced by my stress, exhaustion, and distance. I kept telling myself that these were absurdities and not likely to happen, that next week, Mami would call me and say, "*Hijo, todo está bien. No era nada. Es más, me siento mejor.*"[147] But, as you may already suspect, that was not at all the case for her or me.

---

[146] The Holy Spirit.

[147] Son, everything is good. It wasn't anything. In fact, I feel better.

It was Wednesday. I remember because I taught that day. My day started at 6:00 am on teaching days, Monday, Wednesday, and Friday. I grew accustomed to waking up at that time, sometimes earlier depending on how comfortable I felt with the material I planned to teach that day. My Tropicana early mornings and the endless work shifts that followed have still not turned me into an early morning person, but they have taught me to deal with it.

After teaching, I headed over to Kafe Kerouac, a few blocks from campus. I settled in with a bottomless two-dollar cup of coffee, already on my second or third refill, working on a discussion question for *Native Speaker* by Chang-Rae Lee. The book explores second language acquisition in a style that's both experimental and hardboiled. To be honest, it made me acutely self-conscious about the way I speak English. Accents, after all, are markers of where we come from, shaped by the languages that surround us. They situate us in the world.

I have a Spanish accent, molded by the Dominican dialect of my parents and the Spanish spoken in our neighborhood. I also carry a Brooklyn accent, straight from East New York. And in grad school, I was developing an academic accent, mimicking my professors and classmates, blending into a different linguistic landscape. My accents, combined, gave me a unique identity, but in Ohio, they stood out more than they ever did in Brooklyn. To white people in Ohio, my voice was a point of curiosity, something foreign. Back home, among Black and Latino folks, it wasn't anything remarkable.

I sat in the coffee shop, trying to get through the latter half of *Native Speaker*, but my thoughts kept drifting to Mami. I read about Henry struggling with his detective work and his failing marriage, while also trying to craft a discussion question that wouldn't make me feel even more self-conscious about my English. I took my seminar discussions seriously—maybe too seriously—because English wasn't my first language, and I felt I had so much catching up to do. So, there I was, nervously writing, though I knew my real anxiety was about Mami. I stared blankly into my half-full, sugarless cup of coffee, as if the creamy surface could reveal some kind of answer or truth.

I thought about getting a refill, but before I could stand, my phone buzzed. It was Gabriel, calling at an hour he normally wouldn't. At four in the afternoon, he was usually finishing work or on his way home. I answered, pretending to be casual: "What's up, dude?" His voice broke on the line, and not because of bad reception. His breathing was uneven, heavy. Then he said, "Mami went in for a CAT scan today. The doctors found a big tumor pressing on the left side of her brain."

I could hear the pain in his voice, and I tried not to acknowledge my own, burying it beneath the surface of our conversation. Even though I didn't feel it as acutely as Gabriel did at that moment, the pain started rising in me, slow and suffocating, like a golf ball lodged in my throat. I tried to calm him down, saying the diagnosis could mean many things and that we shouldn't jump to conclusions. I heard it in his voice—his quiet, "Yeah, you think?"—that he was searching for comfort in me, which was rare for him. We hadn't leaned on each other emotionally in years. Our fights and the process of growing up had built a distance between us. Comforting one another wasn't part of our relationship anymore. But this was different. I wanted to be the older brother, if only for this one phone call.

I stayed composed as he continued. Then, almost as if he expected me to know the answer, he asked, "Do you think this is serious? You think Mami's going to die?"

I told him no, that it wasn't serious, even though I knew it was. It was the most serious thing I could imagine. That phone call shifted something in me. I regressed, feeling like I was back in high school, watching myself from the outside, detached. The gray descended deeper over everything that day, heavier and darker than before.

I couldn't cry, not there in the coffee shop, surrounded by people I barely knew. And I was ashamed of that. I was angry. Angry that I couldn't react, that I couldn't break down. It made me feel less human, somehow, for keeping it all inside.

After Gabriel's call, the thought that Mami could die felt so distant, almost unreal. The physical space between me and my family created a buffer, a way to hold back the worst of the fear, though I knew that buffer wouldn't last. I tried to imagine how this grief could manifest into madness, an unraveling of mindfulness into constant panic, first over losing her, then over losing myself in a world without her.

When you're far away, like I was, information comes slowly, medical updates are delayed, emotional support feels diluted. I had to find ways to cope with my own fear and, somehow, my brother's as well, as he began to rely more and more on drugs and alcohol for escape. At the same time, I had to keep myself from losing it.

I told myself that if I didn't double down on my reading, writing, and meditation, I would lose control, become mentally absent from my teaching and coursework. When Mami was hospitalized, her body was overtaken by the tumor,

Gabriel, Julissa, and I bled with fear in our own ways. Few people reached out to us, but I didn't mind the silence. What was happening to Mami—and to us—felt private, too sacred for others to touch.

In the days leading up to Mami's procedure, the dreams of broken teeth stopped. Those messages had already been delivered, manifesting in real life. Out of fear and guilt, I called Mami every day, telling her I loved her more often than I ever had before. I worked myself to exhaustion after classes, only speaking to a handful of people about her condition.

Waiting for the surgery was unbearable. I called Ramiro, Mami's boyfriend at time, to talk through the details, to piece together what the doctors were saying. The tumor was large, but it seemed to be in a part of the brain they could access easily. The doctors were confident, assuring us the surgery would go well. But I wasn't convinced. When the day finally came, I was a mess. I woke up earlier than usual, around 5 a.m., and went through my morning routine as if the repetition could keep my mind from spiraling. I walked to campus, entered the building where I taught my 8 a.m. class, my thoughts racing: *What was the last thing we talked about? When did I last hug her? Did I tell her I loved her?*

The hour before I got any news felt like torture. After class, I went home and broke down. I had a full-blown panic attack, crying face down on my bed, punching the mattress, for an hour until my body ached. I thought about the last conversation I had with her. I spoke to her as if it might be the last time I'd hear her voice. I told her everything I could, what every son with a mother like mine would say: that I wouldn't be the person I am without her, that she taught me resilience, strength, that she was my hero. I told her there would never be another person as loving and selfless as she was. I told her I loved her, that I'd continue my studies, that I'd take care of my brother and sister. And most painfully, I apologized for the hard years I put her through and for not being there by her side now.

At 6 p.m., Julissa finally called. Before I could even say hello, she exclaimed, "She's good, don't worry!" I collapsed onto the bed, feeling as if my own life had been saved. The doctors were able to remove ninety-five percent of the tumor successfully. Weeks later, the prognosis came back: the tumor was benign, with little to no chance of it returning.

Days after the surgery, Mami told me she saw heaven's gates while she was under, and that the angels were singing to her in beautiful voices. She watched them without saying a word, mesmerized by their song. It was their voices, she said, that kept her from waking up. The performance was for her, and she was delighted by the show. Being a singer herself, it felt fitting that an angelic orchestra would serenade her during such a transcendent moment. A few days after the surgery, she wrote a song about the experience.

Un Día Más[148]

Un día más para dar gracias a DIOS
un nuevo día me has dado
y una nueva oportunidad para abrir mi Corazón
y decirle aquí estoy arrepentida, Señor.

---

[148] Lyrics by Ana Luz Peralta.

Tuya soy para abrir mi Corazón
y decirte aquí estoy arrepentida, Señor
tuya soy, gracias, Jesús, gracias, mi DIOS.

Un nuevo día que me has dado
y de la muerte me has librado.

Gracias Jesús, gracias, mi DIOS.
Un nuevo día que me has dado
y de la muerte me has librado.

Te alabaré mientras vida tú me des
y ante ti me postraré para adorarte, mi Señor.

Te alabaré mientras vida tú me des
y ante ti me postraré para adorarte, mi Señor.[149]

---

[149] "One More Day": One more day to thank GOD / a new day you
gave me / and a new opportunity to open my Heart / and to repent,
my Lord. / I am yours to open my heart / and I'll tell you here I am,
repenting, my Lord. / I am yours, thank you Jesus, thank you my
GOD. / A new day you have given me / and you have delivered me
from death. / Thank you Jesus, thank you my GOD. / A new day you
have given me / and you have delivered me from death. / I will praise
you as long as you give me life / and I will submit myself before you to
worship you, my lord. / I will praise you as long as you give me life /
and I will submit myself before you to worship you, my lord.

I was granted a second chance with Mami, and it brought me closer to my family, closer to Gabriel and Julissa. I was certain that from this near-death experience, we'd each learn our own lessons, ones that would, in different ways, strengthen our bond, despite the physical distance between us. But life has a way of twisting things. Though the tumor that attacked Mami didn't take her life, another one came, this time for Papi. Yes, both my parents had brain tumors. And while Mami survived, Papi's was different. His was fatal.

18

Es un buen tipo mi Viejo.

Piero[150]

On April 8, 2019, I defended my dissertation and became the first doctor in my family. The very next day, I buried Papi.

It's impossible to reconcile the significance of these two events happening back-to-back: one, the culmination of a lifetime's work; the other, the sudden loss of the man who made that life possible. Condolences and congratulations poured in, but it all felt like noise. The weight of it didn't settle until a week after the burial, when Papi's grave had hardened and the buzz around my PhD quieted. Only then did I have a moment to reflect.

As irrational as it sounds, sometimes I feel like I traded his life for my degree. For nearly the entire six years of my PhD program, I lived in Columbus, Ohio, 530 miles from Long Island, where Papi lived. During that time, our relationship was put on hold. I thought I had time. He was still young, only in his early fifties, and he didn't smoke or drink excessively. He was an active fisherman, in good physical

---

[150] Piero, "Mi viejo," *Mi viejo* (1969). "He's a good guy, my dad."

shape, with no history of serious illness. I convinced myself that time was something we had plenty of.

By the time I learned Papi was becoming forgetful, losing words, I was in the final stretch of my PhD, buried in revisions for my dissertation. Papi's wife called me one morning in tears, telling me they'd found a tumor. I did my best to calm her, reassuring her that not all tumors are malignant. I told her about Mami's benign brain tumor in 2013 and how she'd recovered. I convinced myself that Papi would be fine and returned to my work. Weeks later, Papi underwent two craniotomies for a biopsy of the tumor on the left side of his brain.

On February 15, 2019, the day after his fifty-third birthday, Papi was diagnosed with glioblastoma (GBM), the most aggressive form of brain cancer. The doctors explained that GBM is ruthless, with no known prevention, and that the median survival time with treatment is twelve to fifteen months. Without treatment, it's only three. Papi died 49 days after his diagnosis.

I was in New York City, interviewing for a tenure-track job at BMCC when I got the news. BMCC felt like a return, not just to New York, but to where my academic journey had begun as an undergrad. In the Uber on my way to the interview, I felt dizzy and nauseous, like there was a tumor growing in my own head.

My partner waited until after the interview to tell me. "Are you done? How did it go?" she asked, calmly. Then: "Can you sit down? I have news." I found myself at the end of city Hall Park Path facing the Brooklyn Bridge and sat on a bench, remembering all the cold and hot days I spent crossing that bridge, camera swinging on my back, trying to photograph my way out of poverty. I watched squirrels and pigeons beg tourists for scraps. "It's glioblastoma," she finally said.

I had already googled the worst types of brain cancer as soon as I'd heard about Papi's condition. So when she said "glioblastoma," I knew he was going to die. I felt the blood in my body coagulate. The sun was bright. The air was cool on the day I found out I would soon be without a father.

After immigrating to this country, we lived in Section-8 housing in East New York, Brooklyn, while Papi delivered food orders on his bicycle across midtown Manhattan. By American standards, we were poor, but in ways that mattered to us, we were rich. Every month, Papi sent money back to Mamá Flora and Papá Victor in the Dominican Republic, the grandparents who raised my brother and me before we left for the U.S.

In the summer of 2018, just five months before Papi's diagnosis, Mamá Flora and Papá Victor were granted travel visas to visit the U.S. for the first time. I remember never seeing Papi happier. Bringing his parents to the U.S. had been his lifelong dream. After nearly three decades apart, they were finally reunited.

At Papi's funeral, my grandmother sat quietly in the front row, staring blankly at his coffin. Through her tears, she softly cried, *"Hijo, tú nos trajiste aquí para dejarnos."*[151]

Papi wasn't perfect. No father is. He beat us, sometimes ruthlessly, in ways I'm still trying to make sense of. I believe he struggled with his own abandonment issues and the trauma

---

[151] "You brought us here, only to leave us."

of his childhood. His biological father left before he was born, a wound he rarely spoke of, partly because of the deep respect he had for Papá Chepe. Though their relationship appeared warm and affectionate, almost ideal on the surface, I wondered if there was still lingering pain in Papi's heart.

Papá Chepe died a year before Papi. I was in Albuquerque, New Mexico, at the biennial conference for the Society for Nineteenth Century Americanists when Papi called me. He was hysterical, like a little boy with air trapped in his throat. He kept repeating, *"Mi papi se murió. Mi papi se murió."*[152] It was heartbreaking, hearing him become a little boy, broken and vulnerable.

To say that Papi spoke little English is an understatement. He didn't really try. But what he lacked in language, he made up for in vibrancy. He was full of life and always stylish. He carried a comb emblazoned with the Dominican flag in his pocket, ready to offer it if your hair needed fixing. Music was part of his very essence. On Sunday mornings, he'd fill our apartment with the sounds of disco from his teenage years or *merengue típico* from his adulthood. He'd even play *güira* on a cheese grater with a fork, pretending to be a *güirero* for Fefita or Los Toros Band.[153]

Though Papi never finished high school, he valued education deeply. In the Dominican countryside where he grew up, school was a privilege, one his family could hardly

---

[152] My daddy is dead. My daddy is dead.

[153] The *güira* is a Dominican percussion instrument made of metal with a textured surface, played by scraping a stiff brush along its side to create a steady, raspy rhythm that anchors merengue and other Afro-Caribbean music.

afford. Mami and my aunts had to take turns going to school because they shared a single uniform and one good pair of shoes. Papi was a bit better off, but even he left school in the ninth grade to help support the family. Despite his limited education, he instilled in my siblings and me the importance of learning. He kept us alive in a neighborhood that felt, at times, like a prison.

Mami and Papi divorced when I was sixteen, and while my siblings and I stayed in Brooklyn, Papi moved to Long Island. He remarried, and though we stayed in touch, the distance between us all grew. In the aftermath of their divorce, we drifted further apart. I turned my focus to trying to be tough, trying to be hood. Gabriel's grades began to slip, and Julissa stopped talking to us altogether. Mami, meanwhile, became more and more afraid. The daily fistfights between Gabriel and me terrified her. She worried that one day, a punch might land on her. She coped the only way she knew how, by calling the cops on me.

Sometimes I'd outrun them, darting out of the house to hide in Stephen's basement or lay low in the corner bodega. Other times, they found me. I'd end up spending a weekend or even Christmas in Central Bookings, crammed in a piss-soaked cell with repeat offenders, listening to them swap stories about how this time they were going to do real time. We'd eat government-issued ham and cheese sandwiches with cartons of milk, waiting for the hours to drag by.

I remember the day I left for graduate school in 2013. Papi visited me in Brooklyn before I left. He parked in front of Mami's apartment, refusing to come inside. We sat in his car and talked about fishing, about Brooklyn and Long Island, about Ohio. We didn't have the typical "going off to college" moment, so this was as close as it got. I told him not to worry about me, that I'd be fine in Ohio. He didn't turn to look at me, but he started to cry. I was caught off guard. When was the last time I'd seen him cry? It had been so long since I felt like a son to anyone. In that moment, I realized how little I really knew him and how little I understood fatherhood.

When we learned the tumor was glioblastoma, my siblings and I rushed to his side. We wanted him to know, even without words, that he was going to be okay. When we arrived at his apartment on Long Island, Papi struggled to rise from his chair, but he was determined to look strong. He wore his favorite sky-blue shirt and jeans. The staples from his surgeries were still fresh on his head. We embraced him all at once, each of us asking for his blessing, *"Ción, Papi."* As always, he replied, *"Que Dios los bendiga, mijos."*[154] It was the first time since my parents' divorce that the three of us—me, Gabriel, and Julissa—were with him under one roof. It took sixteen years and brain cancer for us to share a meal with our father, and that would be our last.

After that, all visits were to Memorial Sloan-Kettering in Manhattan, where he lay bundled under a blanket in a hospital bed. I doubt he fully understood how serious his condition was. The doctors only spoke to us in English, and we had to translate everything for him.

When I asked Papi how he felt, he always said the same thing, *"Muy bien, gracias a Dios."*[155] But I didn't believe him. His mind was slipping. He couldn't remember the year or his

---

[154] May God bless you, my children.

[155] Very good. Thanks to God.

address, but somehow, he always remembered the name of the president. It infuriated me of all the things to remember, why did he hold on to Trump's name?

Papi never talked to me about politics, until Donald Trump was elected. That's when he became afraid. *"Ese hombre, él odia a los inmigrantes,"* he'd say over the phone, half-questioning.[156] *"Ese caco muñeca,"* he'd add, referring to Trump's blond hair, which he thought looked like a troll doll.[157]

The last time I saw Papi alive was over FaceTime. It was April 5, 2019, three days before my dissertation defense. He wasn't taking his chemo meds, and we thought he was just being stubborn. His eyes were blank, his mouth puckered, as Mamá Flora gently moved his head toward her shoulder. I asked him to please take his medicine, my words feeling trite, as if I were talking to a child. I wish I'd said something else, something like, "I'm proud of you. I forgive you. I love you." But I didn't. I told him I had to go, said *"Ción, Papi,"* and ended the call.

He couldn't open his mouth, but I could hear him say, *"Que Dios te bendiga, mijo."* It was the last time I heard his voice.

---

[156] That man, he hates immigrants.

[157] Doll head.

19

Sundays too my father got up early
and put his clothes on in the blueblack cold,
then with cracked hands that ached
from labor in the weekday weather made
banked fires blaze. No one ever thanked him.

Robert Hayden[158]

The opening stanza of Robert Hayden's "Those Winter Sunday" reminds me of Papi, who, no matter the day of the week, was up before the sun at an hour where my dreams were at their deepest, my breath quietest. The "blueblack cold" is the promise of the dawn, before the first glimpse of light. Papi's hands were always cracked, carved by the heavy cold brown cartons he lifted, hardened by the gloveless cold. But as callous and dark as this poem is, it makes me feel like Papi's little boy, warm in my bed, monsters at bay.

Papi is both the hero and the villain of my life's story. He taught me many beautiful things, and many ugly ones too. If there's one lesson Papi drilled into me, it was to work. My first real job was as a bag boy at the local supermarket when I was fifteen. I packed groceries for a couple of dollars, but that

---

[158] Robert Hayden, "Those Winter Sunday" (1962)

didn't last long. I was there one afternoon, doing my thing, when Carlos walked in and spotted me at the end of the counter. He didn't make fun of me. He wasn't about that. My friends weren't the type to shame me for what I didn't have. Carlos and I both knew there was no shame in working. We knew where we came from, who we were, what our parents did, the hard work they put in to keep us going.

I remember Carlos walking up to me after paying for his soda and candy, asking, "My dude, what are you doing working here? You should be outside playing basketball."

He left before I could reply. I stuck around for maybe another hour after that, looking at the cashier, a woman who, tragically, would die in a plane crash later that year on American Airlines Flight 587. I wondered how she did it, day in and day out, without a sigh, with such poise and grace. But me? These few dollars weren't doing anything for my hands, my feet, or my mind. So, I left the store and headed straight to the basketball courts.

My second job was as a different kind of bag boy: a golf caddie. If working at the supermarket made me feel the weight of being a poor immigrant, the Long Island golf course where I caddied made me see privilege in a whole new light. My cousin Romeo and I worked together. It was good money, considering we were two kids from the hood. Romeo was an early riser, never missing that 4:30 a.m. wake-up so we could bike from East New York to Jamaica, Queens, and hop on the Long Island Railroad. The trick was getting to the golf course before the sun came up, before the dew evaporated from the grass. That place felt like a mist: the massive gates, the long, winding road where we rode our bikes while they drove in with their Porsches, Mercedes, and BMWs, headed to the caddie house.

I got to know Romeo through that job. He was awkward then, not tall but still taller than me, always quick-witted with something sharp to say. Honestly, it annoyed the crap out of me. But we were similar, two kids trying to make sense of money and survival in a world that didn't look like ours.

You'd think that seeing my parents struggle with money would have taught me to save. But nope. I was a spendthrift. I blew every dollar I made from the supermarket, the caddie job, and whatever Mami and Papi gave me. Eighty dollars for a full eighteen holes of golf? Gone. I spent it on sneakers, basketball jerseys. This was still the era of throwback jerseys, Mitchell & Ness, and Jordans. Even with all the money I spent, I could never quite keep up with my classmates' gear.

My high school friends thought it was funny, almost bizarre, that a kid from Brooklyn was caddying for white people on Long Island. Like I knew what the fuck golf was. I picked up a thing or two about the game, but what I really learned was that most people who play golf can't actually play golf. They knew all the rules, had the best clubs, and paid for memberships to the most prestigious courses, but skill? That was another story. Golf wasn't really about the game. It was about prestige. And "prestige," I came to understand, was just a fancy way to talk about traditionally white upper-class shit.

When we call something or someone prestigious, we're really talking about exclusion. The high-rolling Wall Street guys and old-money bankers I caddied for pretended their thousand dollar putters were worth it, that it somehow made them better at the game. But I quickly realized it was all nonsense. Being a member of an exclusive golf club wasn't about golf. It was about telling your neighbor, your coworker, your assistant that you belonged to something "elite." It was a titles game, a desperate clinging to prestige, a paying top dollar for an illusion of superiority.

I quickly learned that *that* line of work was not for me. I had never been surrounded by so many white people which made keeping track of their little golf balls and remembering who hit what, who was in the sand trap, who was on the green, and who was still teeing off, incredibly difficult. Romeo somehow managed. In fact, some of those old white guys liked Romeo, requesting him as their caddie, and paid him more than they were "supposed" to. If they like you, you are in fact more valuable: what a commodity that kid was. I was no one's favorite, and there were days when I just did not want to get picked out from the caddie house.

Walking those eighteen holes was no joke. And so, on the days when I felt like doing nothing, most days really, I would hang by the caddie house and watch the teenage girls walk in and out of the clubhouse. Remember, I was sixteen then. And of course, they too were members, but for some reason or another, did not play. Don't get me wrong; some did enjoy the game. They were genuinely excited about slapping white balls with metallic clubs.

These daughters and granddaughters were flirtatious enough to keep me entertained until Romeo was done with his shift. I never pursued any of them though. The attitude of that place made it clear that these weren't my type of people. Rich white entitlement was everywhere like the impenetrable thickness of the early morning fog, the mist Romeo and I rode into every morning, obscuring our vision.

My high school friends knew the deal. I worked to make a little money, just like everyone else, to buy my way into popularity. That was the currency back then, and while people still do it today, it looks different now. But no one went as hard as we did, not like we did. If you were even modestly dressed in our high school, you were easily dropping at least six hundred dollars on an outfit. You'd spend $180 on Nikes (Foamposites or Barkleys), $80 on jeans (Rocawear or Guess), $60 on a shirt (Lacoste or Miskeen), and another $300 on a coat, preferably a North Face. And if you were really trying to stunt, you'd go for high-end designers: Gucci, Prada, Iceberg, Coogi.

We were obsessed with clothes and sneakers, nothing else mattered. At least, I'll admit that for me, it didn't. I was selfish. I didn't think, or maybe I couldn't think, about how hard my parents worked for the little cash they brought home every week. It just wasn't on my radar back then. All that mattered was keeping up with the look.

Some of my friends worked inside the school. I remember George and Nathaniel selling candy during and after school. They made it look cool. They dressed in their newest gear and had regular customers. They posted up by the lunchroom doors, Nathaniel with his box of Oreos and George with fruit snacks. People gravitated toward them, and since eating school lunch was not cool, no one cut their asses for selling candy.

In fact, we all welcomed and thanked these young entrepreneurs for their services, for their hustle. It was a brave move on their parts. Who would have thought that a school driven by the constant blurring of poverty lines and a building of class systems (usually based on clothing) would be somewhat open-minded to candy hustlers?

And I watched them work in awe, wishing I could be that brave. Nowadays, you see that all over the city: young and old men and women alike selling candy and chocolates on the subway to make an extra buck. And no, they are not selling "for a basketball team, just to keep some money in their pockets and stay out of trouble." They always reminded me of my buddies in high school. They reminded me of me and Romeo, and even Mami and Papi getting up early in the "blueblack cold" to make ends meet.

For a long time I believed that a comfortable, successful life came from focusing all your creative energy on making money. What I'm trying to learn is that money should never be the sole goal on my horizon. As Marx writes, "Money is the alienated essence of man's labor and life; and this alien essence dominates him as he worships it."[159] I was raised to worship money, to treat it as a sacred force that gave my life meaning and purpose. Money wasn't just a means to an end. It was the end itself, the thing that supposedly unlocked happiness, security, and respect. It became a false god, shaping how I measured success, how I valued others, and ultimately, how I valued myself.

I was of course not the only one struggling with money. I come from a long tradition of folks who could barely get by. My folks and their folks had been on that money chase way longer than I've been alive, always complaining about not having enough, yet always getting by, feeding and clothing us. Making money was their full time job, at least that was the

---

[159] Karl Marx, *Early Writings* (1975).

way I thought of it. I mean, but how can money be your *telos*? There's no organic backbone to that motivational target.

I used to say to myself that if my folks could not earn money, I was surely not gonna be able to either. Looking at Mami's dishwashing hands, Papi's sunburnt face and calloused palms, I'd say to myself, *I don't think Dominicans are supposed to have money.* And of course, that's ridiculous and entirely inaccurate, especially if you have been to New York City. There's a Dominican bodega on every corner. And then there are those baseball players with million-dollar contracts.

Dominicans have, *dique*, done financially well for themselves in Brooklyn. I couldn't see that though. To me, it was destiny for us to be poor. Destiny was adamant about keeping us unhappy. Was this the life assigned to me? And if so, how could I manage not to be critical of it as I lived through it? How was I going to let life happen to me without losing myself? No. I couldn't let *la pobreza* get me too.[160] I had to fight it for my brother and sister if not for me.

I used to look at Mami and Papi and think to myself, *All they ever talk about is the little money they have and going back to the Dominican Republic.* If they longed for their island so much, my island, why stay here and suffer under the weight of the dollar, under the tyranny of the English language? I never asked them any of these questions. And they never got up and returned to DR. Instead, they coped in their own ways.

On his days off, Papi would sit in front of his "music system," (as he called it), a tower of equalizers, amps, mixers, cassette and CD players, blasting *bachata* and *merengue*, letting the music transport him back. It was as if those rhythms could

---

[160] Poverty.

carry him across time and space, back to the life he left behind in the DR. He worked all week just to come home and relive those moments. His Sunday mornings were sacred, a chance to reclaim a piece of what he'd lost.

"*Allá, todo era diferente. Si uno tenía hambre, uno se come una yautía*," he'd say, reminiscing about the simplicity of life back home.[161]

Many immigrants come to this country for the dollar, and we are quickly dismissed as opportunists. But we don't come here for money alone. The dollar is just a means, a tool to secure our families' futures, to build the hopes and dreams of a better life. The real pursuit isn't wealth. It's the chance to make our dreams a reality.

Papi taught me a lot, but not all of it was good. He beat us regularly with a belt, his fists, or his words. In return, Gabriel and I fought, not knowing how else to communicate. Our fists spoke for us, our anger planted deep, blooming with every disagreement, insult, or slight offense. Fists, headlocks, and scratches filled the air whenever we clashed.

Once, Gabriel and I got into it over who got a turn on the computer. Neither of us would budge. Bart and Pablo were there too, trying to calm us down, knowing how violent things always got in our home. I grabbed the keyboard and smashed it across Gabriel's face, keys flying in every direction. When he recovered, he stormed to the kitchen, grabbed a large knife,

---

[161] There, everything was different. If one was hungry, one could just eat a yautía.

and came straight at me. I ran, and we ended up in the middle of Sunnyside. He jabbed the knife at me, not to stab me, but to scare me. In my mind, though, I had no doubt that he would actually do it. I knew because, if the roles were reversed, I would have done the same.

When Papi found out, he made us strip naked in the bathroom. He ran the shower, took off his belt, soaked it in the water, and beat us until our backs bled.

There was another day, though I can't remember how old I was or what Gabriel and I had done, but we had clearly upset Papi. We begged him for forgiveness, sobbing, promising that we would never do it again. We expected the belt, as usual. But this time, something in his anger felt different. It was calm, almost cold.

"I'm going to do to you what my father used to do to me. This time, you will both learn," he said.

He commanded us to go into the bathroom and step out of our clothes. When he returned, he brought two plates and placed them on the floor next to where we sat, still hiccupping with tears.

I can't bring myself to share what happened next. It's too painful to include in a book about my anger. All I can say is that I had never felt less human than I did that day.

It wasn't until after Papi died that I finally told the story to my partner and my therapist. Only then did I allow myself to fully process it, to think about his words as much as his actions. "What my father used to do to me" lingered in my thoughts for years. It was his confession and commitment. He was passing down the trauma. This is where the hate-love machine becomes useful, hate for what he did to us, but love to heal him for what was done to him. Since then, I've done some healing, and I've forgiven him. But some things, even forgiveness cannot fully erase.

20

People have been trying to kill me since I was born,
a man tells his son, trying to explain
the wisdom of learning a second tongue.

Li-Young Lee[162]

It does feel like death, when someone reminds you that you sound like you're from elsewhere. It's not a death of the flesh, but one of belonging, like you are a ghost in this place, and everyone's afraid.

You don't need an accent to feel like an immigrant. In fact, you don't even have to be an immigrant to experience the alienation that comes with it. If you look like "you aren't from around here," chances are you'll be treated as such. It's becoming painfully clear that the US devalues the lives of migrants and immigrants. Even our politics, on both the left and the right, have grown more conservative when it comes to migrants and immigration.

In 2013, at the age of twenty-five, I became a U.S. citizen. I took the oath on a weekday morning, in a courthouse in Brooklyn, wearing the only blazer I owned. It did not fit well.

---

[162] Li-Young Lee, "Behind My Eyes" (2008).

I stood among dozens of others: Nigerian nurses, Bangladeshi cab drivers, Peruvian line cooks. our bodies bound by our belief in a nation that had asked for much but promised more. When the judge congratulated us and asked us to rise for the national anthem, some people wept. I did not. I imagine that some went out to celebrate with their family and friends. I bought myself a Dunkin' Donuts coffee, and took the local train home.

I had lived in the United States for most of my life with a green card. My family and I arrived in New York City in 1993, when I was six. I still remember the way my mother dressed me that day, in layers, as if to protect me from both the cold and the unknown. It was my first time celebrating Christmas with my father, who had spent years traveling back and forth from DR trying to secure a better life for us. Our migration was, like many, a story of delayed reunions and postponed dreams.

For nearly two decades, I renewed my permanent residency card every eight years. The fee was close to $500, more than I could afford as a student working odd jobs. But I paid it because the cost of not doing so was the greater burden: invisibility, uncertainty, a life half-claimed, and, of course, potential deportation. I became a citizen because I had always felt this country was my home.

Becoming a citizen was not simply about legal status. It was about dignity, about aligning the truth I carried in my bones with the documents in my hands.

According to the Pew Research Center, approximately 24.5 million of the 46.2 million immigrants living in the United States are naturalized citizens, a figure that represents about 53% of all immigrants, based on 2022 estimates from the Migration Policy Institute.[163] It goes without saying—but it must still be said—that the vast majority of us are not criminals. And yet, the Trump administration has made it a political priority to paint us in precisely that light. Since his re-election, Trump has attempted to eliminate birthright citizenship, denaturalize U.S. citizens, and planned to construct "Alligator Alcatraz, an ICE detention center surrounded by alligator-infested waters. With regard to the migrants that the facility would imprison, Trump said, "We're going to teach them how to run away from an alligator if they escape prison."[164] US Secretary of Homeland Security, Kristi Noem, said that "Alligator Alcatraz is the future of immigration enforcement."[165] In these conservative visions, migrants are no longer people. They are a spectacle of suffering, devoured for entertainment and to feed a manufactured sense of white security. Migrants' pain is rendered as performance, their bodies imagined in the jaws of a reptile.

Citizenship, I've learned, is not a static condition. It is always being renegotiated, always subject to the whims of those in power. It is supposed to be permanent, but for naturalized citizens like myself, permanence feels increasingly provisional.

---

[163] Katherine Schaeffer, "1 in 10 Eligible Voters in the U.S. Are Naturalized Citizens." *Pew Research Center* (2024); Migration Policy Institute. *"Naturalized Citizens in the United States." Migration Policy Institute* (last updated in 2024).

[164] Kathryn Watson. "Trump Tours 'Alligator Alcatraz' Immigration Detention Center in Florida." *CBS News* (2025).

[165] Mark Morgan. "Swamp Games: Inside Noem's Controversial 'Alligator Alcatraz' Detention Strategy." *Fox News* (2025).

The Trump administration's attempt to weaponize citizenship is a reminder that we are still in the long shadow of the McCarthy era. In June 2025, the Department of Justice declared that denaturalization would be one of its top five enforcement priorities. Assistant Attorney General Brett A. Shumate issued a memo urging prosecutors to "maximally pursue" such cases, targeting individuals who allegedly misrepresented themselves on their naturalization applications or who have criminal convictions.[166] As NPR reported, this echoes earlier chapters in American history, when people were stripped of citizenship for ideological reasons, during McCarthyism, for alleged communist ties.[167]

This is not 1950. But many of us feel that it could be again. The logic of exclusion, once wielded against political dissidents, now resurfaces in racialized terms, on both sides of the Caribbean. Trump's efforts to eliminate birthright citizenship and denaturalize citizens eerily mirror the devastating policies enacted in the Dominican Republic.

On September 13, 2013, a court decision by the Constitutional Tribunal retroactively stripped citizenship from as many as 245,000 Dominicans of Haitian descent. The court decision overturned the principle of *jus soli,* or birthright citizenship, for the children of foreign-born parents and applied it *retroactively* to 1929.

---

[166] Armando Garcia, "DOJ Looking at Denaturalization for American Citizens Convicted of Certain Crimes." *ABC News* (2025).

[167] Cassandra Burke Robertson, "Denaturalization Is a Tactic That Revives McCarthyism, on Their Citizenship Applications." *NPR* (2025).

This ruling denied birthright citizenship to children born to undocumented Haitian parents, creating a vast stateless population and sparking widespread condemnation. The decision was not just a legal maneuver but a deliberate attempt to exclude and discriminate against a marginalized group. The Center for Migration Studies posits that "Ten years later, as many as 130,000 Dominicans remain stateless and are unable to gain Dominican citizenship, despite the passage of a law in 2014 to correct the court decision and condemnation by the Inter-American Commission on Human Rights."[168] The ruling has resulted in generations of individuals who, despite being born in the Dominican Republic, are denied basic rights and recognition.

The Dominican government continues to heavily prosecute Dominican-born Haitians to control immigration on the Dominican side of Hispaniola. Bureaucratic systems of power, racism, and stereotypes motivate the deportations of Dominican-born Haitians, displacing and separating families and individuals. I know what you might be thinking: *Of course the Dominican government would denaturalize Dominicans of Haitian descent. Dominicans hate Black people.* But you'd be wrong. Most Dominicans do not want this, and there are many individuals and organizations in the Dominican Republic and diaspora fighting oppression and racism.

Organizations like Reconocido, Acción Afro-Dominicana, and MUDHA (Movimiento de Mujeres Domínico-Haitianas) are more than just names. They are

---

[168] Kevin Appleby. "Ten Years After a Fateful Court Decision, the Dominican Republic Still Has a Statelessness Problem." *Center for Migration Studies of New York*, (2023).

lifelines for Black and Haitian communities in the Dominican Republic. These groups push back against a tide of anti-Black discrimination, far-right nationalism, and the brutal deportations that have long targeted Haitians and their descendants. In a country where blackness is often denied and demonized, their work is a fight for dignity, visibility, and survival.

Perhaps it is unsurprising that Trump who built his political career demonizing migrants, associating them with violent crimes and drug trafficking, would support eliminating birthright citizenship and denaturalizing citizens. But these political moves signal a broader hardening of immigration policy.

Migration, in this country, has become a battleground for political point-scoring, rather than a focus of earnest humanitarian concern. This political norm forced Democrats to confront border issues and defend their policies (think about Kamala Harris during her run for president) underscoring a grim reality: the political theater surrounding migration often overshadows substantive solutions.

As I write these words, there is a palpable growing conservative approach to immigration across both major political parties, not just the Republican side. There's a sense that immigrants—particularly undocumented ones or those from mixed-status families—don't have a clear advocate in either party.

I became an US citizen because I believed this country was capable of holding me, and holding itself, accountable. My citizenship ceremony was a moment of celebration, but it was also a prayer, a hope that the country I had chosen would choose me back.

The question now is not whether people like me belong here. The question is what kind of country strips its own of the very thing it promised them in the first place. The answer, I fear, is one we have seen before.

21

¿Dónde estará mi primavera?
¿Dónde se me ha escondido el Sol
Que mi jardín olvidó
Y el alma me marchitó?

Marco Antonio Solís[169]

I thought I was destined to be a Tropicana worker forever, stacking half-gallon cartons in the blueblack of the morning. In New York City, finding work without a degree was tough, so I did what I knew, the job I had watched Papi do for years.

The day always started early, in that eerie hour before the city stirred, when the streets were silent, and it felt like you were the only one awake. I'd crawl out of bed, get dressed, and step out into the cold dark, knowing most of the world was still wrapped in sleep. The Tropicana plant was in Whitestone, Queens, a twisted maze of subway lines and bus routes away from East New York. The commute was a monster—over two hours one way. If I had to be at the plant by 5 a.m., ready to

---

[169] Marco Antonio Solís, "Dónde estará mi primavera," *Más de mi alma* (2001).

load the truck before my boss showed up, I had to be up by 3 a.m. on the dot.

And let's say I worked the day before, clocking out at 6 p.m., exhausted from lifting boxes. By the time I got home after another long bus and train ride, I was already running on fumes. You already know where this is going. There was no way I was getting eight hours of sleep, not in this life. You slept on the train if you were lucky, your head bobbing between the stops, because if you didn't, you might not make it through the next shift.

The lucky ones drove or hitched a ride. My cousin Fernando, long after we patched things up after my *dique* diabolic possession, worked at Tropicana. On good days, I'd ride with him. So on those days, I didn't have to battle the maze of transit lines that seemed designed to break my spirit before the day even began.

Whitestone, Queens, always felt like another world to me. It was this wealthy, almost suburban part of the city, a place where you could see tree-lined streets and those houses you only ever see in holiday movies. It didn't feel like the gritty city I knew. As Fernando pulled into the plant, the whole neighborhood seemed to be asleep. The lights in the houses were off, the streets empty, like the world was still tucked under warm blankets while I was gearing up to lift heavy cartons of juice in the freezing air.

The juice plant loomed ahead, all steel and concrete, set against the backdrop of the Whitestone Bridge. On some mornings, it dazzled with the colors of dawn. Even the most diligent workers would poke their heads out of the truck, if only for a moment, just to feel a brief sense of agency, a reminder that there was purpose behind the grind.

Some of us worked two days in a row, some four days, and others—the unfortunately fortunate ones—worked six and seven days. It was the type of job that exhausted you physically and psychologically. It did not matter how strong you were, how big your muscles were, or how sharp your mind was, this job would take you down after a full day.

All of us "helpers," as they called us, were worn down, broken in by the years of labor. Our backs brittle from endless bending and lifting, our hands calloused, hardened by the constant grip of cartons. The boxes left their mark on us, box after box, day after day. We'd moved millions of them through the five boroughs and Long Island. Our hands had no choice but to toughen up, to become something unfeeling.

It didn't matter how cold it was, how sick you felt, or how tired you felt. You moved those boxes because it was the only way to survive. And when you finally decided you couldn't do it anymore, that was it. Whether you quit or got fired, it made no difference. You'd be replaced in an instant.

Although there were exceptions, most route owners treated their helpers like faceless machines, cogs in the endless grind. No names, no stories, just bodies to keep the work moving. As Ana Castillo might put it, we were the "ideal worker of the semi-legal, exploitative operations of multinational factory production."[170] Cash money softened the blow of this unforgiving whip.

I was fortunate, though, to have worked for some kind route owners. The first was Sean, an Italian man, proud of the life he built, carrying a youthful energy in his charisma. Papi

---

[170] Ana Castillo, *Massacre of the Dreamers* (1994).

had worked for him before I did, and despite not speaking a word of English, he and Sean got along well. In fact, I'm almost certain Sean learned more Spanish in the ten years he worked with Papi than Papi ever learned English from Sean.

The English language never grew in Papi. He struggled with even the simplest words. But that didn't stop him from working. On his route, most of the store owners were Hispanic, so Spanish, New York City's unofficial second language, was all he needed. For Papi, surrounded by Dominicans, there was no real reason to learn English. Why bother when the language you already speak is the one you use every day at work? Truth be told, he didn't try very hard to learn it, either. Like Sean, Papi was a proud man.

I'm sure, like many who learn English later in life, Papi was afraid of sounding foreign, embarrassed to make mistakes. And that's not his fault. English is a cruel illogical language. It's not enough to know the rules or grammar. Second-language learners are expected to iron out their accents, erase the sound of their first tongue until all traces of difference are gone.

For me, the only way that I got through a Tropicana workday was by reading and writing. I always had a book and my journal by my side. *It was my time*, I said to myself, *even if they are paying for it*. But Papi? He only thought about the forty-five twenties he earned at the end of each week. On Fridays, payday, he'd look at me, his eyes red and tired, and say,

"Este trabajo no es fácil, mijo, pero estas cuarenta y cinco papeletas se sienten bien."[171]

The money Papi made halfway impressed me when I was younger. It wasn't until much later, after I had started working for myself—doing the only job he could teach his eldest son—that the image of him holding those forty-five twenties pained me. I began to see how the promise his father had made to him—the American Dream—had fallen by the wayside. How was it that Papi, the firstborn son, was still an immigrant delivery boy, albeit no longer swerving midtown traffic on a bike, while his American-born brother and sisters went to college, earned degrees, and drafted business plans? It was then that I was starting to understand that we were different from them. My aunt and uncles seemed smarter, went to better schools, while Gabriel and I worked alongside Papi at Tropicana, earning untaxed dollars.

When we were younger, Gabriel and I admired our aunts and uncles. Before we grew into rebellious teens and before they became relatively successful professionals, they played significant roles in our childhoods. At eight and ten, we looked up to Papi's siblings; their lives seemed flawless to us. They were real Americans without greencards. They lived in real houses, not in roach-infested buildings. They went to real catholic schools and colleges, not to the regional schools and community colleges. They lived perfectly acculturated American lives, while Gabriel and I, barely managing to defend ourselves with broken English, watched in awe. Their flawless English was a world away from our stumbling tongues,

---

[171] "This work isn't easy, my son, but these forty-five bills feel good."

and with even more distance, we began to wonder about our father.

Money and education have a way of creating divisions within families. Some of us stand at a safe distance, letting the gentle ebb of opportunity lap at our feet, while others, pushed to the frontline, are slammed by waves of responsibility and sacrifice. And we watch, hoping they don't drown.

I realized that Papi never got the chance to focus his energy on something essential to him, on something that gave him purpose, that made him feel alive. He never lived out any dream in the country he traded for his birthplace. The idea that Papi, the worker, might never have had the time or space to contemplate his life, to reflect on his moments, speaks to a deeper truth: he wasn't fully aware that he could. He was too busy surviving to know he was allowed to dream.

Papi's forty-five twenties offered no awareness, no clarity, just survival. Fuck those forty-five bills. Fuck Andrew Jackson. The man who worked hundreds of enslaved people to death in Tennessee, and even now, in the afterlife, his face still poisons men like Papi, pushing them to work without rest. Jackson's face is a monument to the Indigenous people he slaughtered during the War of 1812 and to the violent displacement of entire nations—the Cherokee, Creek, Chickasaw, Choctaw, and Seminole—during what's commonly called the Trail of Tears. But that name isn't accurate. It should be called the Trail of Blood. For many did not simply cry; they died. They collapsed from hunger, exposure, and disease along a brutal journey that stretched over 5,000 miles across multiple forced routes. Entire families buried their elders and children in unmarked graves as they trudged toward an unknown land. Yet here we are, still valuing his image—on the twenty-dollar bill—along with the many others who adorn our currency. But how could Papi know this? How could he, or any of us, grasp the bitter irony of what we worked so hard to earn?

Most of the Tropicana guys were much older than me. They had families, either in New York or back in whatever part of the world they came from, usually Central America. But I wasn't there for anyone else. I was there to make money for myself and spend it just as quickly, the same way I had since my early high school days. But as time passed, my drive began to shift. I kept my eyes open on those long routes, and in the process, I learned more about Papi's life, more about the weight he carried. I saw a glimpse of my own future, and I didn't like what I saw.

Without knowing it, Papi showed me something. He revealed a truth about his life, a brave, humble truth. He was a man who, out of fear or necessity, never learned a new language. I can't resent him for that. I can't resent him for showing me how poor we were, or for teaching me that it takes an exhausting amount of work just to remain poor. That truth was more valuable than any forty-five bills. It was a warning and a lesson wrapped in the quiet dignity of a man who never got to dream beyond survival.

When I was old enough to work on the truck route by myself, things began to change drastically for me. Papi and I partnered for a little while. It felt like a father and son business. Coming into work with him was not work at all unless the real boss was around. Sean was always around, unfortunately. So, my fantasy only played out on the rare occasions when he was out of sight, during the interstices of time when Papi and I walked into stores together, when we organized the truck at the crack of dawn, just us two, father and son.

Papi let me get away with murder at the job. I was his oldest son, so if I was tired, he let me sleep in the passenger seat. If I couldn't lift something, he lifted it for me. Papi, a short man with a lot to prove and even more to give, a man who could still be funny in his daily backbreaking deliveries. This is the man who I found my strength in despite all the suffering, all the trauma and pain.

A year after I began working at Tropicana, Papi had become unhappy with the prospect of working there another day. He was getting older, his back was giving out, and he kept dreaming of a job that was easier on not only his body but his pride. So, he quit.

Papi had sacrificed his pride in front of me daily, so I wouldn't fixate on my own *machismo*. He took orders from younger, taller, wealthier white men, went into stores and was ridiculed at times. He showed me his raw ignorance, the language he couldn't speak, the man he couldn't become, and the precarious dream that got him where he was. It was a brave and dangerous move, and it was all for me. It was then that the concept of livelihood started to outline itself on Papi's face. I saw the deep shades of gray that cradled Papi's eyes, and the creases that, like the pages of worn books, told of mornings and nights of use, reuse and abuse. Pages that were once new and full of interpretive possibilities were growing threadbare and wrinkled.

Of course, I would be misleading you if I said this made sense to me then. I'm only *now* making sense of what those days meant for Papi and me, of the stories he never told me, all he couldn't say. There were days when I hated him for

234

being a working man, for not speaking the language my teachers pretended to have down pat. I remember, more than once, lying about what Papi did for a living, telling my friends in school that he owned a business and made a lot of money.

There were nights when I fell asleep thinking to myself that I was adopted, that my real father was a king somewhere, and that I was left, forgotten by my real parents in the farmlands of the Dominican Republic. These myths and variations like it kept me in a fantasy world and helped me sleep at night. Eventually, the myths that pacified me gutted me

22

Can't get no food to eat.
Can't get no money to spend, Wo-oo-oo.

Burning Spear[172]

It wasn't until after Papi quit and Gabriel and I were living alone at Sunnyside that I really learned the truth about the Tropicana job. Gabriel, barely seventeen, still seemed like he was searching for a place he could call home, while I was just trying to have an apartment of my own. His cool, easygoing nature slowly gave way to anxiety, and I could see it wearing him down. I'm sure the restaurant job had something to do with it.

The restaurant business was brutal, and Gabriel wasn't built for it. The long hours, the constant deliveries down First Avenue, none of it fueled him. The pay was shit too. He told me he hated what he did and wanted out, wanted to find something different. My own work at Tropicana was just as exhausting and depressing, but I knew they were always hiring. I told Gabriel I'd keep an eye out for him. Eventually, an

---

[172] Burning Spear, "Marcus Garvey," *Marcus Garvey* (1975).

opening came up on one of the truck routes, and I referred him to the owner.

At the time, it seemed like a good idea. Gabriel was miserable at the deli, dealing with the endless grind of Manhattan kitchens and the yuppies—or worse, the wannabe yuppies—who loved bossing him around. He was relieved to get away from all that, to escape the snobbery and the suffocating heat of the kitchen.

The Tropicana business brightened Gabriel up again, and everything seemed to be going great in the apartment. Gabriel was making more money and working fewer days, which gave him more time to work on his music but also more time to smoke more cigarettes and blunts.

Gabriel and I got into a rhythm at Tropicana, adjusting to our new life slowly. That winter, Gabriel came down with a cold. It wasn't terrible, but it was strong enough to make him consider staying home from work. Staying home was as simple as having one hundred dollars less in your pocket at the end of the week. I was always under and struggled from month to month with my part of the rent. At times, I would ask Gabriel to let me work one of his days to complete my part of the rent, so I jumped at the opportunity and happily went to work for him the next morning. It had been a few months since Julissa and Mami had moved out, and as the older brother, I also felt responsible for Gabriel.

That day started out early as they usually do when you're in the business of making deliveries to over thirty stores in one day. That morning was normal enough. I knew the route, so delivering and speaking to the store and market owners was not a difficult job. Something was different about that day, however. I won't ever forget the fifth stop of the day, at Marcus

Garvey Houses. As usual, I walked in the store, greeted the owners and everyone who made eye contact with me.

"*Buenas, primo! Tiene la orden preparada?*"[173] I said to the Dominican man behind the counter. I wrote the order down on the flap of a cardboard box I had ripped from one of the hundreds of boxes we kept in the trailer: ten half gallon boxes and three packs of bottled sixteen-ounce apple juice. It was not a lot of merchandise, compared to the large supermarkets, so I completed the order in two trips.

I stacked the juices in the proper order onto the hand truck: the two half-gallon boxes on the base were parallel and faced me, the boxes on top faced the other side and those that followed alternated. It was the only way to deliver three hundred pounds of juice safely on a hand truck across the street and down four uneven steps. A lot can go wrong, trust me. After wheeling the thing inside, I quickly went over the order with the owner and got paid. The only way to make the day's pay feel significant and worth it is by making good time at every store. So, I would always work as fast as I could, doing my best to not get hurt.

That day and that stop was not an exception. By the time I got the order, stacked the juice, and wheeled it in, only ten minutes had passed since Gio, the route owner and driver, stopped the truck and I hopped out of it. After receiving the cash, I walked out of the store with the handtruck in one hand and the other on my hoodie, which I was slipping on to my head. I was cold, and the sun didn't help enough.

---

[173] "Good day, cousin! Do you have the order ready?"

Gio was in the truck making a phone call, probably getting a supermarket delivery order from one of our big stops. To save time, he would sometimes call the stores and get their orders in advance. I unleashed the handle from the side door of the trailer, the metal door swung open, and I lifted the hand truck and placed it on the edge of the trailer.

Before I could close the door, I felt someone behind me. I turned around and a man, maybe twenty-nine or older, stood pointing the barrel of a thirty-eight special at my face. I knew the gun because growing up, my boy Stephen had one just like it. Stephen would bring it over to my block. One time he used a potato as a silencer to muffle the sound and shot into a woodsy vacant lot. Now this same gun was pointed at me. I stopped thinking. I saw myself outside of myself and did not recognize who I was.

He spoke simple English, but my fear prevented me from understanding his words.

"You already know what it is!" he blurted.

I was as still as the wind that winter morning.

He repeated, "You already know what it is, son!"

And I, in utter shock, looked to him as if to make sense of what was happening to me. I looked into his dark eyes and at the buck fifty that ran across his face from his hairline to his lip slit. He was a pained man, who cared very little, and worse yet, I did not know him, and this was really happening to me.

"Run all of your shit," he continued.

I did as I was told. I gave him the money I had collected in the store, but it was not enough for him. He was not at all interested in the petty change. He knew the Tropicana business, apparently, and asked for the safe.

"I want it all! Where's the safe?" said the man whose loose finger wrapped even tighter around the trigger.

I didn't see a potato on the barrel of his piece. My death was going to be loud and then silent, at least that's how I think it would've been.

"It's . . . it's—in the front of the truck," I stuttered.

"Yo, word to everything, Imma kill you if you don't get me that safe."

He said he would kill me if I didn't get the money for him, and there wasn't a doubt in my mind that he meant it. My life meant nothing to him. I've always feared being murdered. I remember feeling this intense urgency inside me to beg him, to tell him that I didn't own the truck, that I was broke, so broke I didn't know what to do with myself. I wanted to tell him I was an immigrant, that I wasn't even a citizen, that I could be evicted at any moment.

But nothing came out. Not a word. Not a peep. Instead, my mind went to different places: to Jagua and *la casita en el campo*, to those *tigres* who doubted my *dique* Dominican-ness in La Yagüita de Pastor, to the showdown with the Crips on Utica Ave. I returned to the present moment: to this scarred man pointing his glistening .38 at me. He held the gun loosely now, in the closed palm of his right hand. He was ready to escort me to the realm of the non-flesh.

I thought, *I'm only twenty. I'll disappoint my brother. I'll die without apologizing to Mami and Julissa. I'll die without saying goodbye to Papi.*

My lungs filled with air, and I finally released: "The rest of the money is in the safe, and that's in the truck," my voice, shaken, foreign. Gio was in the truck. The side trailer door partially blocked his view. I wondered, I wonder still, if he knew I was at risk of losing my life.

"Hey, boss man!" the gunman yelled. "Come out here. I have a business deal for you."

"What you want?" Gio replied, in his cool Bergen Beach English.

"I know a store that wants service, come out here and talk to me." The gunman was good at improvising lines and keeping calm.

"I'm not interested in the store," Gio replied, but what I heard, in my mind, was, "You can kill him. He's worthless."

I couldn't read the gunman's emotions. He didn't seem to care that Gio was still sitting in the truck. He pressed the gun to my chest. It felt heavy and cold, like it was vacuuming my soul through the barrel. He demanded again, this time more forcefully, that I give him all the money I had. Without waiting for my response, he reached into my wallet and helped himself to the rent money I'd planned to deposit later that evening. His frustration was clear. He wasn't satisfied with what he found.

He told me to get in the truck anyway. I turned slowly, not daring to look back. I was six feet from the passenger door, but to me, it felt like the full extent of my life. I walked, feeling the cold barrel stare—lingering at the base of my neck. My mind flashed to Mami, my sister, then Gabriel and Papi. *This is it*, I thought. *This man is going to end my life right here, in front of the Marcus Garvey Houses, with my back turned, for a few hundred dollars.*

Perhaps it was ironic—perhaps fate—that the robbery happened right in front of a project building named after

Marcus Garvey, the Jamaican Black nationalist and pan-Africanist. Garvey's vision was bold and radical for its time. He rejected the assimilationist ideals that painted America as a melting pot, instead advocating for the political and economic unification of all people of African descent. He believed in a future where Black people would achieve financial independence and liberation from the oppressive systems that sustained white supremacy. His words called for empowerment, self-reliance, and dignity.

I imagine the gunman, a Black man not yet 30, caught in the very cycle of poverty and oppression that Garvey warned against. The gunman wasn't just robbing me; he was taking from a system that had already taken so much from him. I was just collateral, standing in the way of his survival. The irony isn't lost on me now. But back then, as I was living it under the shadow of Garvey's name, all I could think about was my life.

I opened the truck's door, got in, and closed it as quietly as possible, while the gunman casually walked back into the building like nothing had happened.

"What happened?" Gio asked, his voice barely cutting through the fog of my thoughts.

"I was held up," I said, my voice strange, like it didn't belong to me. Gio muttered something under his breath as we drove to the next stop, but I wasn't listening. I found an odd sense of relief in the fact that Gabriel wasn't there, that he didn't have to go through this. I was working his shift. He was supposed to be the one on this route. That thought calmed me, as if I had taken the hit for him, and in some twisted way, that made it easier to bear.

We continued the route like nothing had happened. As the truck moved along the streets, I picked up the book I had been reading, James Baldwin's *Another Country*. Baldwin's words pulled me in, offering a strange comfort even as my insides still trembled. Reading was my ritual, my way of coping, and I matched the rhythm of the juice stops with pages turned, using Baldwin's storyworld to drown out the chaos of my own. His world wasn't mine. It wasn't even his, really. He told me this:

> The occurrence of an event is not the same thing as knowing what it is that one has lived through. Most people had not lived—nor could it, for that matter, be said that they had died—through any of their terrible events. They had simply been stunned by the hammer. They passed their lives thereafter in a kind of limbo of denied and unexamined pain. The great question that faced him this morning was whether or not he had ever, really, been present at his life.[174]

I read on, hands shaking but never lifting my eyes from the page. I was becoming a reader, not just someone who skimmed words, but someone who truly inhabited them. The world of books became my refuge, a place where I could lay down the weight of what had just happened, of all the things that would happen, of all I'd carried for years.

From that day on, I read more books. I claimed them, consumed them, trying to replace my traumas with new words, new stories, new worlds. It wasn't that I was erasing what I'd been through, but that I was starting to reshape it, to give it language and meaning.

---

[174] James Baldwin, *Another Country*, (1962).

I was finally claiming the words that had kept Mami and Papi silent for so long, words that had made them feel voiceless, countryless. And in doing so, I was finding my own voice, my own country.

That cold morning, in some strange, unexpected way, the gunman had given me something too. He hadn't just taken my money. He had pushed me toward a truth I hadn't yet understood: that I could either be stunned by the hammer, or I could lift my head, look the world in the eye, and keep reading, keep living.

Peace.

ABOUT AYENDY BONIFACIO

Ayendy Bonifacio (he/him/his) is the author of *To the River, We Are Migrants: Poems/Poemas* (2020), *Paratextuality in Anglophone and Hispanophone Poems in the US Press, 1855-1901*, as well as the forthcoming novel, *Bless Me, Papi* (2026). His writing has appeared in *The New York Times*, *Slate*, and *The Los Angeles Review of Books (LARB)*. Bonifacio is an associate professor of English at the University of Toledo in Ohio, where he lives with his partner and daughter.

ABOUT THE PRESS

Unsolicited Press is based out of Portland, Oregon and focuses on the works of the unsung and underrepresented. As a womxn–owned, all–volunteer small publisher that doesn't worry about profits as much as championing exceptional literature, we have the privilege of partnering with authors skirting the fringes of the lit world. We've worked with emerging and award–winning authors such as Sommer Schafer, Amy Shimshon–Santo, Brook Bhagat, Mari Matthias, and Amy Baskin.

Learn more at Unsolicitedpress.com. Find us on Twitter and Instagram at @UnsolicitedP.

www.ingramcontent.com/pod-product-compliance
Lightning Source LLC
Chambersburg PA
CBHW031456120626
46545CB00005B/1633